TECHNICAL REPORT

The Effect of the Assessment of Recruit Motivation and Strength (ARMS) Program on Army Accessions and Attrition

David S. Loughran • Bruce R. Orvis

Prepared for the United States Army

Approved for public release; distribution unlimited

RAND ARROYO CENTER

The research described in this report was sponsored by the United States Army under Contract No. W74V8H-06-C-0001.

Library of Congress Control Number: 2011938328

ISBN: 978-0-8330-5313-8

Published 2011 by the RAND Corporation
1776 Main Street, P.O. Box 2138, Santa Monica, CA 90407-2138
1200 South Hayes Street, Arlington, VA 22202-5050
4570 Fifth Avenue, Suite 600, Pittsburgh, PA 15213-2665
RAND URL: http://www.rand.org/
To order RAND documents or to obtain additional information, contact
Distribution Services: Telephone: (310) 451-7002;
Fax: (310) 451-6915; Email: order@rand.org

Preface

The fraction of American youth meeting U.S. Army enlistment standards for weight and body fat has decreased markedly over the past three decades. In response to this adverse trend, in February 2005, the Army allowed six Military Entrance Processing Stations (MEPS) to grant an enlistment waiver to applicants who exceeded weight and body fat standards as long as they passed a physical endurance, motivation, and strength test known as the Assessment of Recruit Motivation and Strength (ARMS) test. ARMS was developed by medical scientists at the Walter Reed Army Institute of Research who believed that it complements existing physical fitness tests used to evaluate potential military enlistees. The Army implemented ARMS at eight additional MEPS in February 2006 and at the remaining 51 MEPS in April 2006. This report examines the effect on Army accessions and attrition of granting enlistment waivers to applicants who pass the ARMS test. It will be of interest to policymakers, military manpower analysts, and clinicians concerned about the effect of America's obesity epidemic on the ability of the military services to access and retain a healthy and productive enlisted force.

This research was sponsored by the Assistant Secretary of the Army for Manpower and Reserve Affairs at the request of the Office of Accession Policy, and it was conducted within the RAND Arroyo Center's Manpower and Training Program. RAND Arroyo Center, part of the RAND Corporation, is a federally funded research and development center sponsored by the United States Army.

The Project Unique Identification Code (PUIC) for the project that produced this document is SAMRS06963.

For more information on RAND Arroyo Center, contact the Director of Operations (telephone 310-393-0411, extension 6419; FAX 310-451-6952; email Marcy_Agmon@rand.org), or visit Arroyo's web site at http://www.rand.org/ard/.

Contents

Figures

Tables

Summary

In February 2005, the U.S. Army allowed six Military Entrance Processing Station (MEPS) locations—Atlanta, Buffalo, Chicago, Sacramento, San Antonio, and San Diego—to enlist Army applicants who did not meet applicable weight-for-height and body fat percentage standards but who passed a test known as the Assessment of Recruit Motivation and Strength (ARMS) test.[1] ARMS has two components: a step test and a pushup test (initially, it also had a lift component). Successfully completing these tests is meant to indicate that a recruit has the physical and motivational endurance needed to serve in the Army. The Army expanded the use of the ARMS test to eight additional MEPS in February 2006 and to the remaining 51 MEPS in April 2006.

The decision to allow ARMS waivers nationwide was made in a difficult recruiting environment and at a time when the Army was seeking to grow active-duty end strength. The decision was also made with the knowledge that America's obesity epidemic was adversely affecting the supply of eligible recruits and with the belief that ARMS complements existing physical fitness tests used to identify individuals who will and will not fare well in the military. According to data available from the Military Entrance Processing Command, between 1988 and 2007, the mean body mass index (BMI) of Army male applicants increased from 23.8 to 24.9, and the mean BMI of female applicants increased from 22.3 to 23.9 (Figures S.1 and S.2). Even-larger increases in BMI are apparent among the heaviest applicants. For example, BMI at the 75th percentile of the applicant BMI distribution increased from 26.1 to 27.7 for males and from 23.8 to 25.9 for females. BMI in the overall U.S. youth population increased by even more during this period (Asch et al., 2009).

The Army granted waivers to overweight and over–body fat applicants who passed the ARMS test, hoping that this would increase enlistments without adversely affecting attrition and other measures of recruit readiness. The research reported in this document investigates whether implementation of ARMS succeeded in meeting this goal by examining military personnel data obtained from the Military Entrance Processing Command and the United States Army Accessions Command on nearly 260,000 individuals who applied to the Army between 2004 and 2007.

Methods

One way to measure the effect of ARMS on accessions would be simply to count the number of Army recruits who enlisted with an ARMS waiver. However, there are two main reasons why this measure is not likely to provide a reasonable estimate of the effect of ARMS on Army

[1] Hereafter, we use *weight standards* to refer to *weight-for-height standards*.

Figure S.1
Cumulative Distribution of BMI, by Year: Males

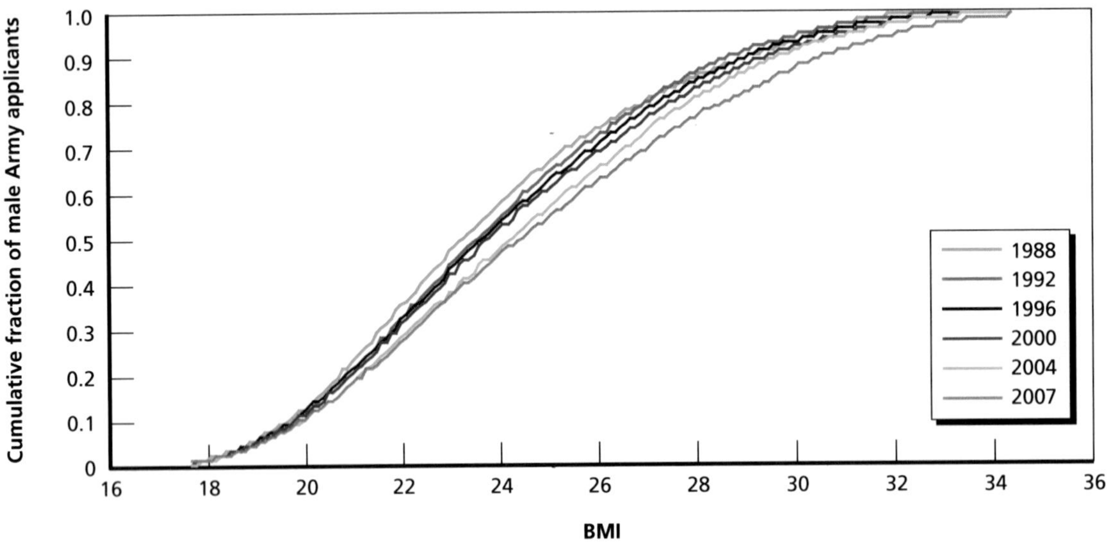

NOTES: The sample is restricted to non–prior service (NPS) regular Army male applicants with valid weight and height measurements. Weight and height are as recorded at the applicant's first medical exam.
RAND *TR975-S.1*

Figure S.2
Cumulative Distribution of BMI, by Year: Females

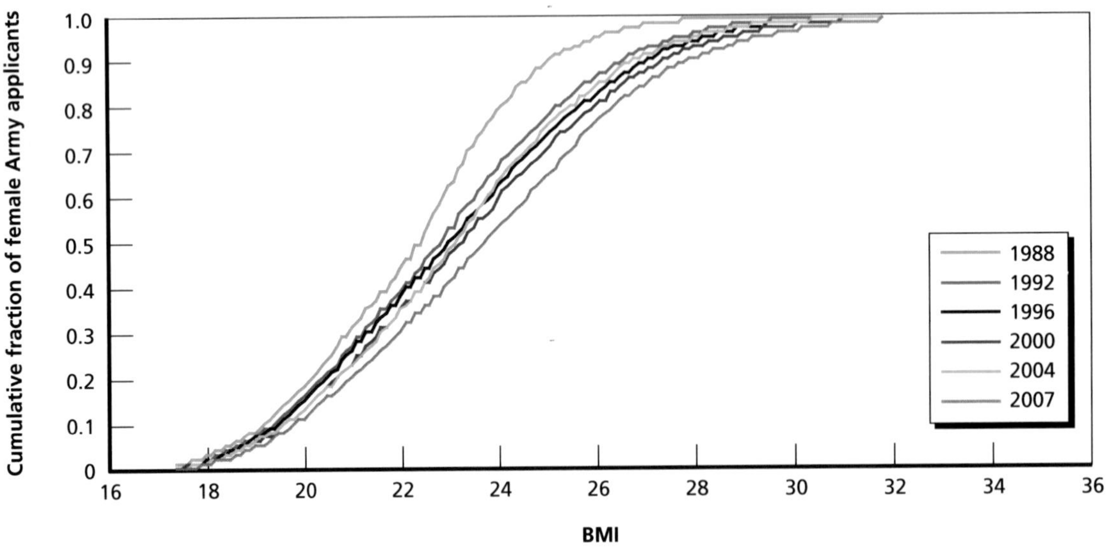

NOTES: The sample is restricted to NPS regular Army female applicants with valid weight and height measurements. Weight and height are as recorded at the applicant's first medical exam.
RAND *TR975-S.2*

accessions. First, Army recruits who fail weight and body fat standards at their first medical exam are allowed to return at a later date for retesting. Our data indicate that, before ARMS was implemented, about 45 percent of Army applicants who initially failed weight and body fat standards later met those standards, and 89 percent of those applicants accessed within 30 days of their last physical exam. Thus, it seems likely that some fraction of recruits who enlisted with an ARMS waiver would have enlisted in the absence of ARMS by losing the weight and body fat necessary to meet Army standards. Second, it is possible that the availability of ARMS had a broader effect than just increasing the number of accessions of recruits who failed to meet weight and body fat standards. The availability of ARMS might have encouraged some individuals who were overweight but within body fat standards to apply when they might otherwise not have.

To capture the full effect of ARMS on accessions, we compared changes in accessions over time at a set of MEPS that did implement ARMS with changes at a set of MEPS that did not implement the test. This difference-in-differences approach assumes that the accession experience of MEPS that did not implement ARMS can serve as the counterfactual experience of MEPS that did implement ARMS (i.e., that the former would have been the experience of the latter had the latter not implemented ARMS).

The reader will recall that ARMS was first implemented at six MEPS in February 2005. These six MEPS were the only MEPS authorized to grant ARMS waivers to overweight and over–body fat applicants between February 2005 and January 2006. Thus, our approach was to compare the change in accessions between 2004 and 2005 at the six ARMS study sites with the change in accessions between 2004 and 2005 at the other 59 MEPS.

The Effect of ARMS on Army Accessions

The difference-in-differences estimate of the effect of ARMS on Army accessions is most easily understood in simple tabular form. In section A of Table S.1, we see that male accessions occurring within 30 days of the last observed medical exam fell by 11.6 percent between 2004 and 2005 in nonstudy sites but increased by 6.6 percent in study sites.[2] This means that accessions in study sites increased by 6.6 – (–11.6) = 18.3 percent relative to nonstudy sites during that period. Female accessions in study sites increased by 24 percent relative to nonstudy sites. In section B, we see that this relative increase in accessions at study sites was not attributable to a relative increase in the accession rate. In fact, our data indicate that the accession rate in study sites fell relative to nonstudy sites between 2004 and 2005. This suggests that the relative growth in accessions must have been attributable to a relative increase in applications, which is exactly what we see in section C. Male applications at study sites grew by 21 percent relative to nonstudy sites between 2004 and 2005, and female applications grew by 28 percent.

It is notable that the relative growth in both applicants and accessions at ARMS study sites was primarily among overweight applicants and accessions. Male and female overweight but within–body fat applications at the ARMS study sites grew by 21 and 30 percent, respectively, relative to the nonstudy sites (section E). Male and female over–body fat application at the ARMS study sites increased by 268 and 197 percent, respectively, relative to the nonstudy

---

[2] All counts are expressed in natural logs. The difference in these log counts approximate percentage changes. Here, the difference rounds to 18.3 percent.

Table S.1
Change in Application and Accession Outcomes Between 2004 and 2005 Across Nonstudy and Study Sites, by Gender

	Change in Outcome Between 2004 and 2005	
	Males	**Females**
A. Ln(Accessions)		
Nonstudy sites	−0.116	−0.225
Study sites	0.066	0.014
Δ	0.183*	0.239*
B. Accession rate		
Nonstudy sites	−0.012	0.001
Study sites	−0.030	−0.022
Δ	−0.018	−0.023
C. Ln(Applicants)		
Nonstudy sites	−0.100	−0.227
Study sites	0.106	0.048
Δ	0.206*	0.275*
D. Ln(Within-weight applicants)		
Nonstudy sites	−0.107	−0.241
Study sites	−0.021	−0.202
Δ	0.085	0.039
E. Ln(Overweight but within–body fat applicants)		
Nonstudy sites	−0.073	−0.173
Study sites	0.136	0.126
Δ	0.210*	0.300*
F. Ln(Over–body fat applicants)		
Nonstudy sites	−0.010	−0.364
Study sites	2.668	1.603
Δ	2.678*	1.967*
G. Ln(Within-weight accessions)		
Nonstudy sites	−0.116	−0.234
Study sites	−0.045	−0.236
Δ	0.071	−0.002

Table S.1—Continued

	Change in Outcome Between 2004 and 2005	
	Males	**Females**
H. Ln(Overweight but within–body fat accessions)		
Nonstudy sites	−0.121	−0.209
Study sites	0.094	0.138
Δ	0.215*	0.347*
I. Ln(Over–body fat accessions)		
Nonstudy sites	0.378	0.182
Study sites	4.019	3.226
Δ	3.640*	3.043*
J. Category I-IIIA rate		
Nonstudy sites	−0.081	−0.089
Study sites	−0.078	−0.074
Δ	0.002	0.015
Number of observations	108,862	24,173

NOTES: The sample is restricted to NPS regular Army applicants who received their last observed medical exam between February 2004 and January 2006. Chapter Two describes additional sample restrictions. Category I-IIIA recruits are those scoring at or above the 50th percentile of the Armed Forces Qualification Test distribution.

* The difference is statistically significant at the 1-percent confidence level.

sites (section F). Note also that within-weight applications at ARMS study sites grew relative to nonstudy sites (section D), although by a substantially smaller amount (8.5 and 3.9 percentage points for males and females, respectively) than overweight applications. The same pattern is evident when we examine accessions (sections G, H, and I). Finally, section J shows that the strong relative increase in the number of overweight and over–body fat applications at ARMS study sites was not correlated with a change in the Armed Forces Qualification Test (AFQT): The percentage of Category I-IIIA recruits fell by about 8 percentage points at both the study and nonstudy sites.

We examined the robustness of the findings reported in Table S.1 by controlling for differences in local economic conditions and recruiting resources and for the possibility that some of the relative growth in applications and accessions at ARMS study sites was attributable to the fact that these sites drew applicants and accessions away from nearby MEPS. The basic pattern of results, however, is unaffected by these considerations: The number of overweight applications and accessions, but not the accession rate, grew strongly at ARMS study sites relative to nonstudy sites between 2004 and 2005. Taking these factors into account, our estimate is that ARMS increased overweight but within–body fat male (female) accessions by 13 (26) percent and overweight and over–body fat male (female) accessions by 350 (192) percent. Overall, our estimates imply that ARMS increased overweight male (female) accessions by 35 (62) percent. These estimates also imply that ARMS had no statistically significant effect on the number of within-weight Army applicants or accessions.

The Effect of ARMS on Army Attrition

Our analyses suggest that ARMS was effective in increasing accessions, but did that increase in accessions come at the cost of higher attrition? To answer this question, we began by examining how 6- and 18-month attrition rates varied with weight and body fat as measured at an applicant's first medical exam and whether that applicant passed the ARMS test. Table S.2 shows that attrition rates were elevated among overweight but within–body fat male enlistees. For example, in this sample, the 6-month attrition rate of male enlistees who were more than 15 pounds overweight at the time of their first medical exam was 7.5 percent, compared with an average of 5.5 percent for within-weight enlistees. Table S.2 further shows that 6-month attrition rates were even higher among over–body fat male enlistees who either did not take or failed the ARMS test (8.0 and 9.0 percent, respectively). However, of great significance is the fact that the attrition rate of over–body fat male enlistees who passed the ARMS test was not statistically different from the attrition rate of within-weight enlistees. The 18-month attrition rate of female enlistees who passed ARMS was actually somewhat lower than the 18-month attrition rate of within-weight female enlistees. These data suggest that the ARMS test is effective at identifying over–body fat applicants who are as likely to complete initial training as within-weight applicants.

Although it would appear from the results reported in Table S.2 that overweight enlistees who passed ARMS had relatively low attrition rates, it is not clear from this evidence alone that ARMS results in lower attrition rates overall. We know that accessions increased in study sites relative to nonstudy sites and that those accessions were disproportionately overweight and over–body fat. The net effect of this change in the composition of accessions on attrition rates is unclear. On the one hand, attrition was higher among overweight accessions, which

Table S.2
Attrition Rates, by Gender and Weight and Body Fat Percentage Relative to Army Standards: FY 2007

Weight and Body Fat Relative to Army Standards	Males			Females		
	6-Month Attrition Rate	18-Month Attrition Rate	*Number of Observations*	6-Month Attrition Rate	18-Month Attrition Rate	*Number of Observations*
Within-weight	0.055	0.145	55,635	0.104	0.294	8,201
1–15 lbs overweight, within–body fat	0.060	0.144	5,703	0.102	0.278	1,598
>15 lbs overweight, within–body fat	0.075*	0.159*	6,731	0.113	0.292	1,108
>0 lbs overweight, not within–body fat, no ARMS test	0.080*	0.169**	1,129	0.083	0.261	399
Failed ARMS	0.090*	0.180*	645	0.155**	0.361***	155
Passed ARMS	0.064	0.141	1,251	0.092	0.256**	644

NOTES: The sample is restricted to NPS regular Army enlistees who received their last observed medical exam between October 2006 and September 2007 and accessed within 30 days of that exam. Chapter Two describes additional sample restrictions. Weight and body fat are as recorded at the applicant's first medical exam.

* Statistically different from the attrition rate of within-weight enlistees at the 1-percent confidence level.

** Statistically different from the attrition rate of within-weight enlistees at the 5-percent confidence level.

*** Statistically different from the attrition rate of within-weight enlistees at the 10-percent confidence level.

would tend to increase attrition rates under the ARMS program. On the other hand, attrition was lower among overweight accessions who passed the ARMS test. Thus, to the extent that ARMS screens out applicants who might otherwise have accessed and separated, ARMS could result in lower overall attrition rates. To test whether ARMS affected overall attrition in the six study sites, we employed the same difference-in-differences framework we used to study accessions. These difference-in-differences estimates suggest that ARMS had no net effect on male or female attrition rates either in the overall accession population or in the population of overweight accessions.

Although we find that ARMS had no effect on attrition rates, it is nonetheless possible that those who accessed through an ARMS waiver separated for different reasons than those who did not. In particular, it might be the case that ARMS accessions were more susceptible to injury than their non-ARMS counterparts and were therefore more likely to separate for medical reasons. However, an analysis of separation codes available in our administrative data suggest that male accessions who passed the ARMS test and separated within 18 months of accession were somewhat less likely than within-weight accessions to separate for medical reasons but somewhat more likely to separate because they did not meet physical (e.g., weight and body fat) standards (see Table S.3). Curiously, the same was true of male accessions who failed the ARMS test and so presumably met weight standards prior to accession. Female accessions who took the ARMS test prior to accession were also less likely than within-weight accessions

Table S.3
Reason for Separation, by Gender and Weight and Body Fat Percentage Relative to Army Standards: FY 2007

	Reason for Separation				
Accession Category	**Medical**	**Physical Standards**	**Conduct**	**Other**	***Number of Observations***
A. Males					
Within-weight	0.210	0.174	0.507	0.098	8,066
Overweight, within–body fat	0.232*	0.217*	0.422*	0.107	1,893
Over–body fat, no ARMS test	0.236	0.267*	0.393*	0.105	191
Failed ARMS	0.147*	0.259*	0.457	0.112	116
Passed ARMS	0.182	0.244*	0.432*	0.119	176
B. Females					
Within-weight	0.236	0.174	0.276	0.295	2,410
Overweight, within–body fat	0.243	0.189	0.287	0.280	767
Over–body fat, no ARMS test	0.346*	0.154	0.183*	0.308	104
Failed ARMS	0.107*	0.143	0.429*	0.304	56
Passed ARMS	0.164*	0.188	0.291	0.345	165

NOTES: The sample is restricted to NPS regular Army enlistees who received their last observed medical exam between October 2006 and September 2007, accessed within 30 days of that exam, and separated within 18 months of accession. Chapter Two describes additional sample restrictions. Weight and body fat are as recorded at the applicant's first medical exam.

* The difference from the within-weight mean is statistically significant at the 5-percent confidence level.

to separate for medical reasons. This evidence, then, suggests that, if anything, ARMS accessions were less susceptible than non-ARMS accessions to injury that resulted in separation. However, it might still be the case that ARMS accessions were more likely than non-ARMS accessions to suffer other types of injuries, including those that impede performance but do not result in separation. We did not have access to data that would allow us to investigate this issue.

Conclusion

When the Army implemented ARMS at the six study sites in 2005 and then at the remaining MEPS in 2006, the hope was that the test would increase accessions among overweight and over–body fat applicants without adversely affecting attrition. The evidence reported here suggests that implementation of ARMS at the six study sites succeeded in doing just that. Our difference-in-differences estimates imply that the implementation of ARMS increased male accessions by 13 percent and female accessions by 20 percent in 2005 and that virtually all of that percentage increase came from overweight and over–body fat accessions. Despite the fact that ARMS resulted in a large increase in the proportion of applicants who were overweight and over–body fat, our estimates imply that ARMS had no effect on attrition rates. This suggests that the ARMS test is effective in identifying overweight and over–body fat recruits who are as likely as within-standards recruits to complete initial training. Moreover, ARMS has been quite inexpensive to implement. Our estimates imply that the cost of ARMS per additional accession was $163 in fiscal year 2007, which compares very favorably with the estimated per-accession cost of other Army recruiting initiatives.

We temper this overall conclusion with several caveats. First, we cannot say for certain whether the broader implementation of ARMS since 2005 has been as successful as it was at the six study sites. However, at a minimum, the available evidence indicates that overweight and over–body fat applicants who pass ARMS are no more likely to separate than are applicants who meet weight and body fat standards. Second, it remains to be seen whether ARMS accessions in the longer run will turn out to be as productive on average as within-standards accessions. Although our tabulations suggest that ARMS accessions are, if anything, somewhat less likely than non-ARMS accessions to separate for medical reasons, it may be that they are more prone to injuries (e.g., heat illness, musculoskeletal injury) that do not result in separation but that make these accessions less productive. Moreover, it is important to acknowledge that ARMS appears to increase the number of overweight but within–body fat accessions. These individuals would not be subject to the ARMS test, and our evidence suggests that they are somewhat less likely than within-weight recruits to complete initial training.

The decision to implement ARMS was made in a weak recruiting environment. Today, the recruiting environment is much stronger (largely because of the weak civilian labor market), and, as a result, the Army decided to suspend ARMS as of October 2009. However, even in a very strong recruiting environment like the current one, ARMS can serve a highly useful role by identifying enlistees who, despite weight problems, can be productive members of the Army enlisted force. The success of the ARMS test suggests what might appear obvious in hindsight: The population of overweight and over–body fat individuals is quite heterogeneous. Some of these individuals are truly unfit for service, but many others possess the desire and ability to serve their country in the armed forces and, given the chance, will succeed in that capacity. In both weak and strong recruiting environments, then, the ARMS test offers a simple, cost-effective way to separate the fit from the unfit.

Acknowledgments

This research would not have been possible without the assistance of dedicated staff within the Army, the Office of the Secretary of Defense (OSD), and RAND. The offices of the Assistant Secretary of the Army for Manpower and Reserve Affairs; Deputy Chief of Staff, G-1; and OSD/Accession Policy provided guidance and support throughout the project. We are grateful to LTC Holly West (then of United States Army Accessions Command), Kevin Dupont (U.S. Military Entrance Processing Command), and Maris Michaels (Defense Manpower Data Center) for helping us obtain and interpret the military personnel and health data used in this research. We are indebted to Colonel David Niebuhr of the Walter Reed Army Institute of Research and to Christine Eibner of RAND for providing insightful reviews that substantially improved this research. We also benefited from conversations with knowledgeable staff at the Pittsburgh MEPS, the Cleveland MEPS, and the Los Angeles MEPS. We thank Major Eric Martinez (OSD/Accession Policy) for organizing visits to those MEPS. Finally, we thank Laurie McDonald, Craig Martin, and Janet Hanley at RAND for providing superior programming support.

Abbreviations

AIM	Assessment of Individual Motivation
AFQT	Armed Forces Qualification Test
ARMS	Assessment of Recruit Motivation and Strength
BMI	body mass index
FY	fiscal year
Ln	natural log
MEPS	Military Entrance Processing Station
NPS	non–prior service
OSD	Office of the Secretary of Defense

CHAPTER ONE

Introduction

The U.S. Army screens applicants on a variety of dimensions, including weight and body fat. Prior to 2005, applicants who did not meet age- and gender-specific weight-for-height and body fat standards were ineligible to enlist.[1] For example, an 18-year-old non–prior service (NPS) male measuring 5 feet 10 inches passed weight standards if he weighed less than 190 pounds. (See Appendix A for a complete tabulation of Army weight and body fat enlistment standards by age and gender.) Applicants who exceeded weight standards were still eligible to enlist, provided that their body fat percentage did not exceed limits that varied with age and gender.[2] For the applicant just referenced, the body fat limit would have been 24 percent.

It is well known that the U.S. youth population has grown substantially heavier over the past several decades. Asch et al. (2009), for example, find that the mean weight of males and females ages 17–21, conditional on height, increased by 12.5 and 10.3 pounds, respectively, between 1980 and 2001. The fraction of American youth who meet Army weight standards has fallen substantially. Asch et al. (2009) estimate that, in 2001, 79 and 63 percent of white males and females ages 17–21, respectively, met Army weight standards. Among African American and Hispanic youth, the percentage meeting Army weight standards was even lower. Although a higher fraction of youth meet applicable body fat standards, it is clear that weight and body fat standards substantially limit the pool of qualified Army applicants and that the weight-eligible pool has decreased markedly in just a few decades.

In 2005, the Army, under a Walter Reed Army Institute of Research Institutional Research Board–approved research protocol, allowed six Military Entrance Processing Stations (MEPS) locations—Atlanta, Buffalo, Chicago, Sacramento, San Antonio, and San Diego—to admit certain overweight and over–body fat Army applicants who passed the Assessment of Recruit Motivation and Strength (ARMS) test.[3] The ARMS test employed at these six study sites was designed as part of a study that sought to identify simple metrics that could be used to determine whether an individual possesses the physical fitness and motivation necessary to complete basic combat training (Niebuhr et al., 2008).[4] ARMS has two components: a step test, which

[1] Hereafter, we use *weight standards* to refer to *weight-for-height standards.*

[2] Body fat percentage is approximated by a formula based on weight, height, and the circumference of the neck, abdomen, and (for women) hips (see Headquarters, Department of the Army, 2006). Weight and body fat content standards are stricter for applicants with prior military service.

[3] Male (female) applicants whose body fat percentage exceeded 30 (36) percent were not eligible for the ARMS test. This maximum body fat standard was increased to 32 (38) percentage points in April 2009.

[4] ARMS is one of several tests developed by the Army in recent years in an effort to improve applicant screening. Others include the Assessment of Individual Motivation (AIM), a 27-item, self-administered questionnaire designed to measure six temperament constructs relevant to military performance (dependability, adjustment, physical conditioning, leader-

measures fitness and motivation, and a pushup test, which measures muscular endurance.[5] The step test requires applicants to step up to and down from a 12-inch step at a cadence of 120 beats per minute for five minutes.[6] Each step with each leg represents one beat, so the cadence requires applicants to step up to and down from the step 30 times a minute. A metronome audible to the applicant maintains the cadence. The pushup test requires male (female) applicants to complete a minimum of 15 (4) pushups in one minute.[7] Failure to complete either component results in failure of the ARMS test.

The ARMS test was first piloted at the six study sites in February 2004, although it was not used to screen applicants for enlistment at that time. In February 2005, the Army directed the six study sites to grant waivers to applicants who passed the ARMS test. Then, in February 2006, the Army expanded use of the ARMS test to eight additional MEPS. Finally, in April 2006, the Army expanded use of the ARMS test to the remaining 51 MEPS. However, in October 2009, with the recruiting environment improving due to a weakening civilian labor market, and with recruiting budgets coming under pressure, the Army decided to suspend ARMS.[8]

The decision to allow ARMS waivers nationwide was made in response to the need to grow Army active-duty end strength in a difficult recruiting environment. The decision was also made in recognition that America's obesity epidemic was adversely affecting the supply of eligible recruits. Specifically, it was hoped that allowing waivers for overweight and over–body fat applicants who passed the ARMS test would increase enlistments but that doing so would not result in a larger fraction of enlistees who fail to complete initial training or otherwise leave service prematurely. There is only one published study that begins to assess results against these goals. Niebuhr et al. (2008) employed ARMS test pilot data collected in 2004 from the six study sites to test whether applicants who passed ARMS were less likely to separate during initial training than applicants who did not pass the test. Conditional on applicant age, race/ethnicity, BMI, and smoking history, they find ARMS test performance to be significantly related to the risk of attrition within 180 days of enlistment. Their estimates imply that failing the ARMS test increases the likelihood of male and female attrition by 36 and 127 percent, respectively. Niebuhr et al. (2009) further demonstrate that individuals accessing with an ARMS waiver between February 2005 and September 2006 were no more likely than those who met weight and body fat standards to separate within 180 days of accession. Bedno et al. (2010a, 2010b), however, report a higher incidence of heat illness among ARMS recruits and a slightly higher 15-month attrition rate.

Thus, research to date suggests that the ARMS test provides a useful measure of physical fitness in both the overall and overweight or over–body fat recruit populations. This report complements existing studies by examining the effect of ARMS on accessions and by presenting alternative analyses of the effect of ARMS on attrition. Chapter Two provides an overview

ship, work orientation, and agreeableness), and the Tier Two Attrition Screen for non–high school graduates, which is a composite measure of AIM, Armed Services Vocational Aptitude Battery, and body mass index (BMI) scores. BMI can be computed by dividing weight (in kilograms) by the square of height (in meters).

5 Originally, ARMS also contained a dynamic lift test. This element of the test did not contribute measurably to the screening power of the ARMS and thus was eliminated.

6 The step height for males was reduced to 12 inches from 16 inches in April 2009; it was 16 inches during our study.

7 See Niebuhr et al., 2008, for a more thorough description of the ARMS test and its development.

8 Email communication with Don Bohn, United States Army Accessions Command, February 2, 2010.

of the data sources employed in our study and defines our analysis sample. Chapter Three reports basic statistics on trends in weight and body fat in the Army applicant population and a variety of statistics related to ARMS test performance for applicants who took the test between February 2006 and September 2007. Chapters Four and Five report the results of analyses of the effect of ARMS on Army applications, accessions, and attrition. Chapter Six discusses the policy implications of our findings.

CHAPTER TWO

Medical History and ARMS Data

This report employs administrative data on Army applicants and enlistees from a number of sources. The construction of our analysis file began with an extract from the Medical History File,[1] which records data on each physical exam administered to Army applicants, including the applicant's height, weight, and body fat percentage. As discussed in Chapter Four, a substantial percentage of Army applicants who fail weight and body fat standards during their first physical exam meet these standards at a later date. Therefore, it was critical that we had data on all physical exams rather than just the last physical exam, which is what is contained on standard applicant extracts generated by the Military Entrance Processing Command. We obtained additional information about these applicants from the Defense Manpower Data Center in the form of a file containing data on all military applicants.[2] These additional data items include the applicant's MEPS location, service applied to, score on the Armed Forces Qualification Test (AFQT), prior service, race/ethnicity, and home county of record.

Into this file we merged detailed information on ARMS-related test scores for applicants who took the test between February 2006 (when the ARMS test was expanded beyond the six initial study sites to eight additional MEPS) and December 2007.[3] These scores cover all applicants who took the ARMS test during this period, except applicants who took the test at one of the six study sites; in the case of study-site applicants, our data contained scores for those who took the test between September 2006 and December 2007. Finally, we merged into our file data on accessions and separations from a file known as RA Analyst, which we obtained from the U.S. Army Accessions Command. The data we extracted from RA Analyst contain information on enlisted accessions through December 2009.

Our merged file contains records for 287,063 NPS applicants to the regular Army whose first medical exam occurred between January 1, 2004, and September 30, 2007.[4] We reduced this sample to 257,763 applicants, mostly because data on weight, height, and body fat were lacking but also because we lacked data on the other covariates just described. We also dropped a small number of applicants whose height did not conform to minimum and maximum height standards, whose medical history exam dates did not accord with dates recorded in the ARMS data, or whose accession and medical exam dates indicate that the individual accessed before his or her last medical exam.

[1] These data were obtained from Kevin DuPont, Military Entrance Processing Command, in January 2007.

[2] These data were obtained from Marisa Michaels, Defense Manpower Data Center, in April 2009.

[3] We obtained these ARMS data from LTC Holly West, United States Army Accessions Command, in July 2008.

[4] We dropped a small number of applicants (< 0.01 percent) whose records reflected more than three medical exams or more than two ARMS tests.

Table 2.1 shows, by month, the number of NPS regular Army applicants in our analysis file. As can be seen, the annual number of applications varied significantly over the study period in our sample, from 81,088 in 2004 to 65,715 in 2005 and 68,312 in 2006.[5] Table 2.2 shows, by month and year of last medical exam, the fraction of applicants who accessed within 30 days of their last physical exam and the fraction of these accessions who separated within 18 months of accession.[6] Of note is the decline in the 18-month separation rate over this period, from 22 percent to 16 percent between 2004 and 2007.[7]

Descriptive statistics for our sample of NPS regular Army applicants are reported in Table 2.3. The sample was 83 percent male and 67 percent white. The average age of the applicants was 21 years, and the average AFQT percentile score was 58. Average height was 5 feet 9 inches, and average weight was 163 pounds. The average body fat percentage of applicants whose body fat was measured—body fat is measured only if the applicant is overweight—was 25.3.

Table 2.1
Number of Regular Army NPS Applicants Who Received a Medical Exam and Took ARMS, by Month and Year of First Physical Exam

	First Exam: 2004		First Exam: 2005		First Exam: 2006		First Exam: 2007	
Month	Applicants	ARMS	Applicants	ARMS	Applicants	ARMS	Applicants	ARMS
1	6,177	0	4,811	0	5,751	0	5,272	294
2	5,676	0	4,793	0	4,751	65	4,507	251
3	6,904	0	5,072	0	5,669	51	5,132	255
4	6,714	0	4,770	0	5,422	291	4,292	259
5	5,934	0	4,152	0	5,962	249	3,986	215
6	8,856	0	6,112	0	7,008	266	4,434	204
7	8,292	0	5,997	0	5,909	246	4,662	227
8	8,717	0	7,157	0	7,347	301	5,675	241
9	9,307	0	6,607	0	6,054	240	4,688	229
10	5,635	0	5,378	0	5,176	291	No data	No data
11	4,326	0	5,353	0	4,634	268	No data	No data
12	4,550	0	5,513	0	4,629	199	No data	No data
Total	81,088	0	65,715	0	68,312	2,467	42,648	2,175

NOTES: The sample is restricted to NPS regular Army applicants who received a medical exam for the first time between January 2004 and September 2007. The text describes additional sample restrictions.

[5] Accessions and applications dropped after 2004 due to a combination of factors, including challenging recruiting times that required faster shipping of applicants to training and an increase in the proportion of prior-service recruits.

[6] About 96 percent of the applicants who accessed in our sample accessed within 30 days of their last medical exam; 89 percent accessed on the same day as their last medical exam.

[7] During this period, the seniority of approval authority for early separation was increased. This change, together with other factors (such as an emphasis on remedial actions during training when needed), was associated with a reduction in the early attrition rate.

Table 2.2
30-Day Accession Rate and 18-Month Attrition Rate, by Month and Year of Last Physical Exam

	Last Exam: 2004		Last Exam: 2005		Last Exam: 2006		Last Exam: 2007	
Month	Accession	Attrition	Accession	Attrition	Accession	Attrition	Accession	Attrition
1	0.74	0.21	0.75	0.20	0.77	0.16	0.80	0.18
2	0.75	0.24	0.69	0.20	0.74	0.16	0.73	0.19
3	0.75	0.24	0.70	0.21	0.69	0.17	0.69	0.18
4	0.72	0.25	0.65	0.22	0.71	0.17	0.68	0.19
5	0.74	0.23	0.72	0.17	0.70	0.17	0.72	0.18
6	0.79	0.20	0.80	0.14	0.78	0.15	0.70	0.16
7	0.77	0.18	0.79	0.14	0.80	0.13	0.72	0.15
8	0.74	0.21	0.77	0.16	0.80	0.16	0.66	0.16
9	0.80	0.23	0.76	0.16	0.70	0.18	0.59	0.17
10	0.72	0.24	0.70	0.16	0.71	0.19	0.88	0.19
11	0.72	0.27	0.73	0.19	0.72	0.22	0.83	0.22
12	0.51	0.20	0.47	0.14	0.06	0.11	0.23	0.13
Average	0.74	0.22	0.73	0.17	0.73	0.16	0.71	0.17

NOTES: The sample is restricted to NPS regular Army applicants who received a medical exam for the first time between January 2004 and September 2007. The text describes additional sample restrictions. The 30-day accession rate is the fraction of applicants who accessed within 30 days of their last medical exam. The 18-month separation rate is the fraction of accessions who separated within 18 months of accession, conditional on accessing within 30 days of their last medical exam.

Table 2.3
Descriptive Statistics

Variable	Mean	Standard Deviation
A. Males		
Age	20.8	3.9
Race		
White	0.687	—
Black	0.131	—
Other	0.057	—
Unknown	0.125	—
AFQT percentile	59.2	20.7
Height (inches)	69.6	2.7
Weight (pounds)	168.5	31.7
Body fat measured	0.213	—
Body fat percentage	23.6	3.4

Table 2.3—Continued

Variable	Mean	Standard Deviation
Took the ARMS test	0.016	—
Accessed within 30 days	0.743	—
Separated within 6 months	0.080	—
Separated within 18 months	0.161	—
Number of observations	213,649	—
B. Females		
Age	20.7	4.2
Race		
White	0.597	—
Black	0.203	—
Other	0.081	—
Unknown	0.119	—
AFQT percentile	55.0	19.4
Height (inches)	64.4	2.5
Weight (pounds)	134.9	22.6
Body fat measured	0.315	—
Body fat percent	30.6	3.2
Took the ARMS test	0.029	—
Accessed within 30 days	0.664	—
Separated within 6 months	0.149	—
Separated within 18 months	0.310	—
Number of observations	44,114	—

NOTES: The sample is restricted to NPS regular Army applicants who received a medical exam for the first time between January 2004 and September 2007. The text describes additional sample restrictions. The 6- and 18-month separation rates are conditional on accessing within 30 days of the last medical exam.

CHAPTER THREE

Trends in Body Fat Percentage and the ARMS Test

With the ARMS test, otherwise qualified Army applicants could access in one of three ways:

1. meeting applicable weight standards
2. meeting applicable body fat standards
3. passing the ARMS test.[1]

In this chapter, we begin by providing background statistics on the fraction of Army enlistees potentially subject to ARMS testing. We then supply detailed statistics on the characteristics of ARMS applicants who did and did not successfully complete the test.

Trends in the Body Fat Percentage of Army Applicants

It is well known that American youth have become heavier over the past several decades, so it is perhaps unsurprising that the Army applicant pool has also become substantially heavier. According to available Military Entrance Processing Command data, between 1988 and 2007, the mean BMI of Army male applicants increased from 23.8 to 24.9; mean female BMI increased from 22.3 to 23.9. As Figures 3.1 and 3.2 demonstrate, BMI increased more strongly among the heaviest applicants. For example, BMI at the 75th percentile of the applicant BMI distribution increased from 26.1 to 27.7 for males and from 23.8 to 25.9 for females.

Our data contain body fat measurements only for the years 2004–2007 and only for applicants who exceeded weight standards; as noted earlier, body fat is measured only if the applicant is overweight. These data indicate a very large increase in body fat percentage between 2004 and 2007. For example, the mean body fat percentage of male Army applicants ages 17–20 increased from 21.7 to 24.2 between 2004 and 2007 (see Table 3.1). For female applicants ages 17–20, mean body fat percentage increased from 28.8 to 32.0.

This increase in the body fat percentage of Army applicants over the course of just a few years is substantial. There are a number of potential explanations for this increase, but it is worth noting that a very large increase in body fat percentage occurred among applicants ages 17–20 between June and July 2005. This increase in body fat percentage can be seen in Figures 3.3 and 3.4, which graph the cumulative distribution of body fat percentage among overweight male and female applicants ages 17–20 in May–June 2005 and in July–August 2005.

[1] As Chapter Four relates, available data suggest that a small number of overweight and over–body fat applicants accessed without passing ARMS. In principle, this is not allowed, and so it might be that these individuals were in fact within-weight or within–body fat at the time of accession or had in fact passed ARMS even though available data indicate otherwise.

Figure 3.1
Cumulative Distribution of BMI, by Year: Males

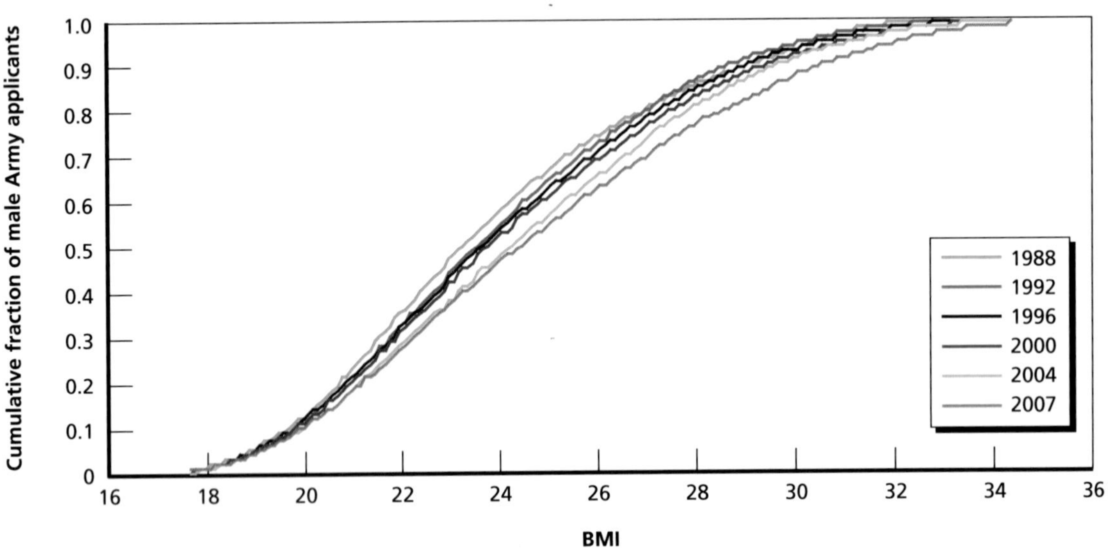

NOTES: The sample is restricted to non–prior service (NPS) regular Army male applicants with valid weight and height measurements. Weight and height are as recorded at the applicant's first medical exam.
RAND *TR975-3.1*

Figure 3.2
Cumulative Distribution of BMI, by Year: Females

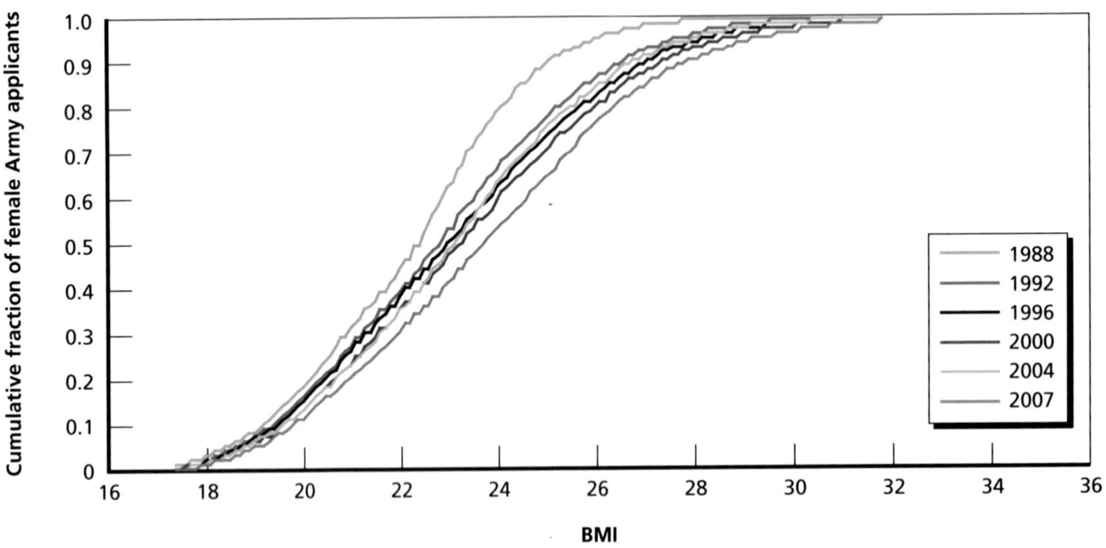

NOTES: The sample is restricted to NPS regular Army female applicants with valid weight and height measurements. Weight and height are as recorded at the applicant's first medical exam.
RAND *TR975-3.2*

Table 3.1
Mean Body Fat Percentage of Overweight Applicants, by Gender, Age, and Period

	Period				
Gender and Age	**2004**	**Jan–Jun 2005**	**Jul–Dec 2005**	**2006**	**2007**
A. Males					
17–20	21.7	22.7	23.5	24.1	24.2
21–27	22.9	23.6	23.8	24.4	24.4
28–39	24.4	24.9	25.0	25.2	25.0
B. Females					
17–20	28.8	29.4	30.1	30.8	32.0
21–27	30.4	30.9	31.2	31.4	32.7
28–39	31.8	31.7	32.2	32.3	33.6

NOTES: The sample is restricted to overweight NPS regular Army applicants age 39 or younger who received a medical exam for the first time between January 2004 and September 2007. Chapter Two describes additional sample restrictions. Body fat is as recorded at the applicant's first medical exam.

Figure 3.3
Cumulative Distribution of Body Fat Percentage in May–August 2005: Males, Ages 17–20

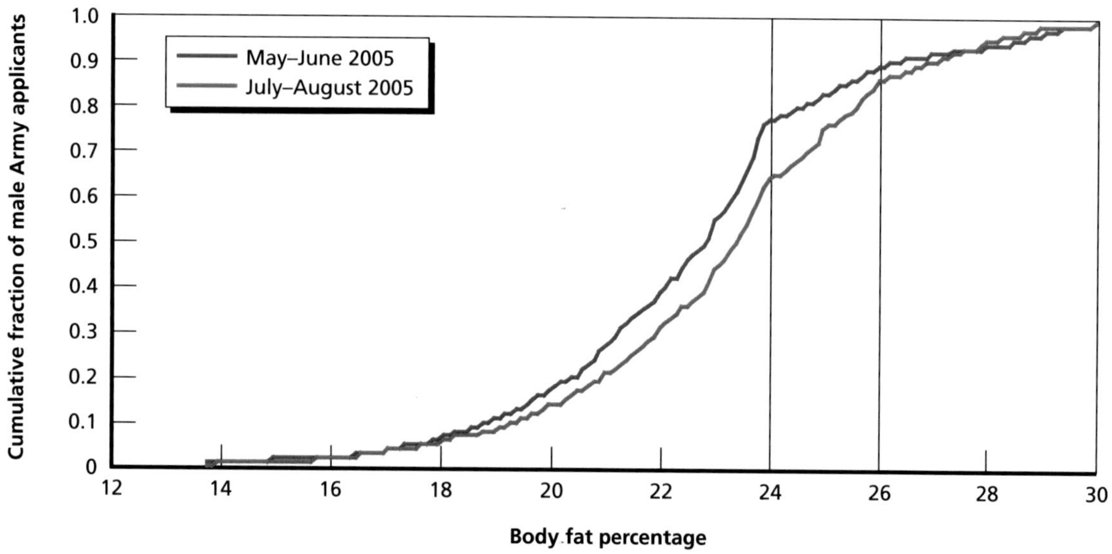

NOTES: The sample is restricted to overweight NPS regular Army male applicants who received a medical exam for the first time between May and August 2005. Chapter Two describes additional sample restrictions. Body fat percentage is as recorded at the applicant's first medical exam.
RAND *TR975-3.3*

Figure 3.4
Cumulative Distribution of Body Fat Percentage in May–August 2005: Females, Ages 17–20

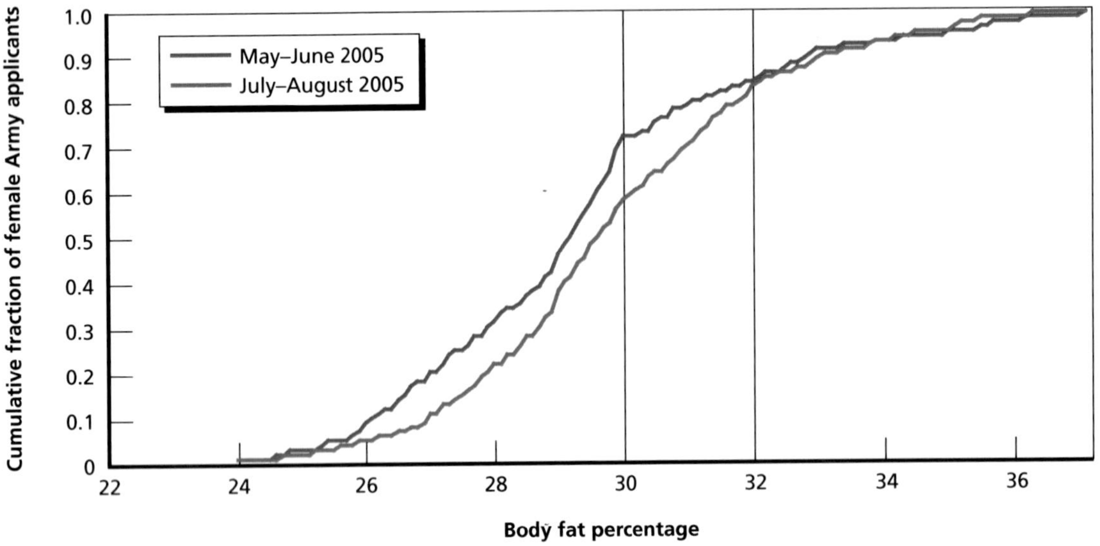

NOTES: The sample is restricted to overweight NPS regular Army female applicants who received a medical exam for the first time between May and August 2005. Chapter Two describes additional sample restrictions. Body fat percentage is as recorded at the applicant's first medical exam.
RAND *TR975-3.4*

There is no evidence of such a sharp change in the body fat distribution of older male recruits between May–June 2005 and July–August 2005 (see Figure 3.5), although Figure 3.6 suggests that the body fat percentage of older female recruits increased somewhat over that same period.

It is highly unlikely that the body fat distribution of younger Army applicants changed so much in the span of a single month in the absence of a change in Army standards.[2] According to Army Regulation 40-501, *Standards of Medical Fitness*, the Army officially increased the permissible body fat percentage for male applicants ages 17–20 from 24 to 26 and for female applicants ages 17–20 from 30 to 32 on June 27, 2006 (Headquarters, Department of the Army, 2007). However, available accession data suggest that MEPS locations in fact implemented the new body fat standards in July 2005.

In Figure 3.7, we show, by body fat percentage (as measured at the last physical exam), the percentage of overweight male applicants ages 17–20 who accessed within 30 days of their last physical exam. This figure does not include data for applicants in the six ARMS study sites; thus, the possible direct influence of ARMS on accession standards in 2005 is removed. In May and June 2005, we see that the fraction accessing with a body fat percentage of 24 or less was between 80 and 90 percent. The fraction accessing declined sharply at body fat percentages above 24, suggesting that a body fat percentage of 24 was the effective standard during those months. In July and August of 2005, we see a very small decrease in accessions at the official body fat standard of 24 and then a large decrease in accessions above the body fat percentage of 26. The same shift in accessions between May–June 2005 and July–August 2005 is apparent among female applicants ages 17–20 (Figure 3.8) but not among male and female

2 Another possible explanation is that the procedure for measuring body fat changed between these two months, but we have no evidence that such a change occurred.

Figure 3.5
Cumulative Distribution of Body Fat Percentage in May–August 2005: Males, Ages 21–27

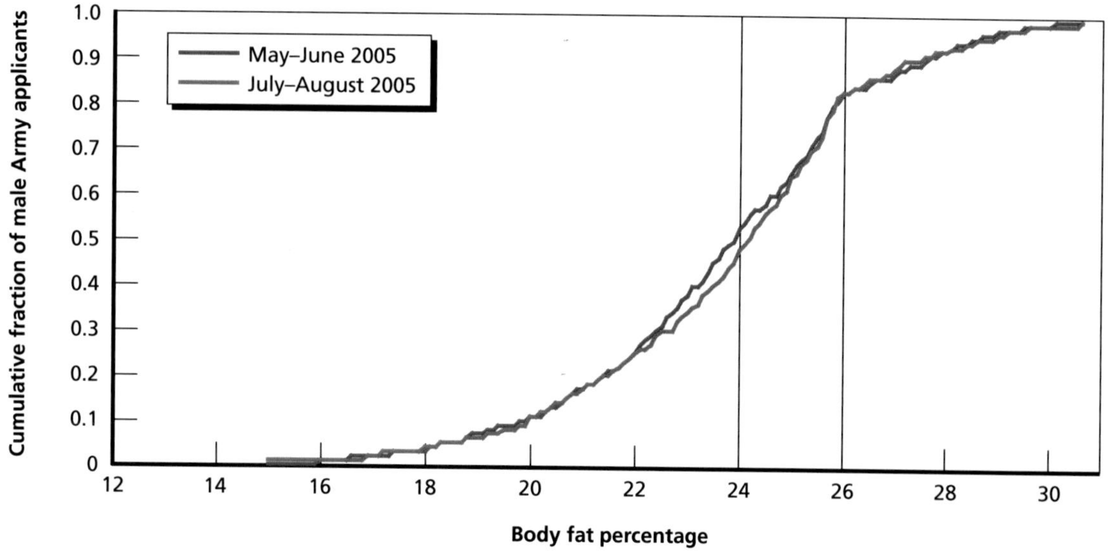

NOTES: The sample is restricted to overweight NPS regular Army male applicants who received a medical exam for the first time between May and August 2005. Chapter Two describes additional sample restrictions. Body fat percentage is as recorded at the applicant's first medical exam.
RAND *TR975-3.5*

Figure 3.6
Cumulative Distribution of Body Fat Percentage in May–August 2005: Females, Ages 21–27

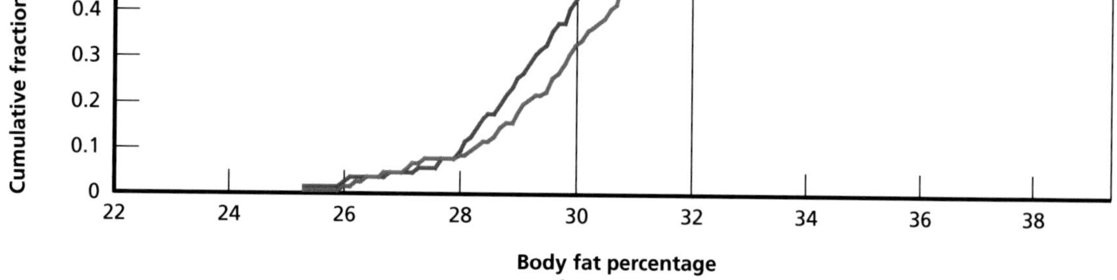

NOTES: The sample is restricted to overweight NPS regular Army female applicants who received a medical exam for the first time between May and August 2005. Chapter Two describes additional sample restrictions. Body fat percentage is as recorded at the applicant's first medical exam.
RAND *TR975-3.6*

Figure 3.7
30-Day Accession Rate, by Body Fat Percentage, in May–August 2005: Overweight Males, Ages 17–20

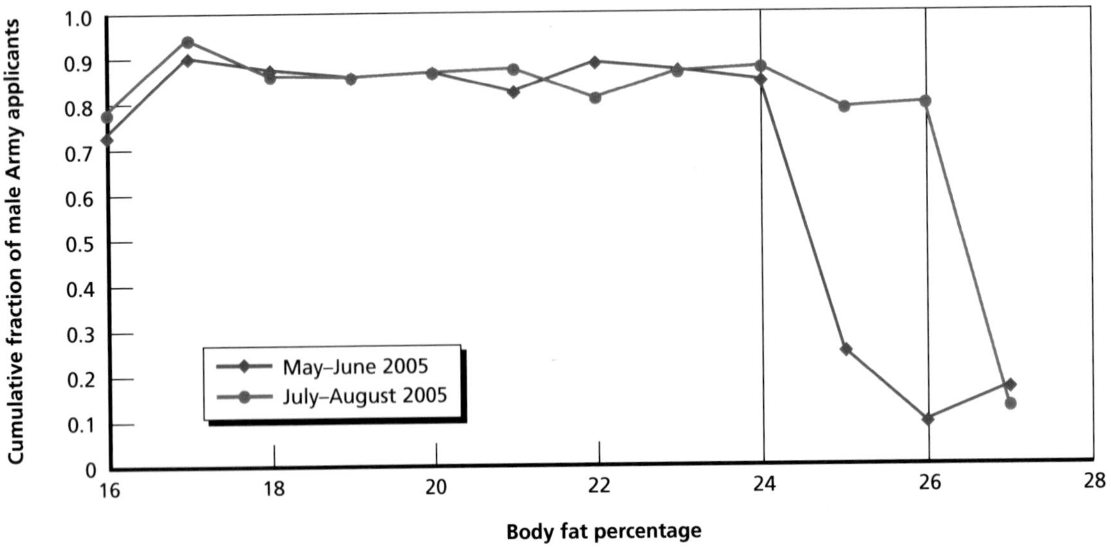

NOTES: The sample is restricted to overweight NPS regular Army male applicants who received their last observed medical exam between May and August 2005. The sample does not include applicants processed by one of the six ARMS study sites. Chapter Two describes additional sample restrictions. Body fat percentage is as recorded at the applicant's last observed medical exam.

RAND *TR975-3.7*

Figure 3.8
30-Day Accession Rate, by Body Fat Percentage, in May–August 2005: Overweight Females, Ages 17–20

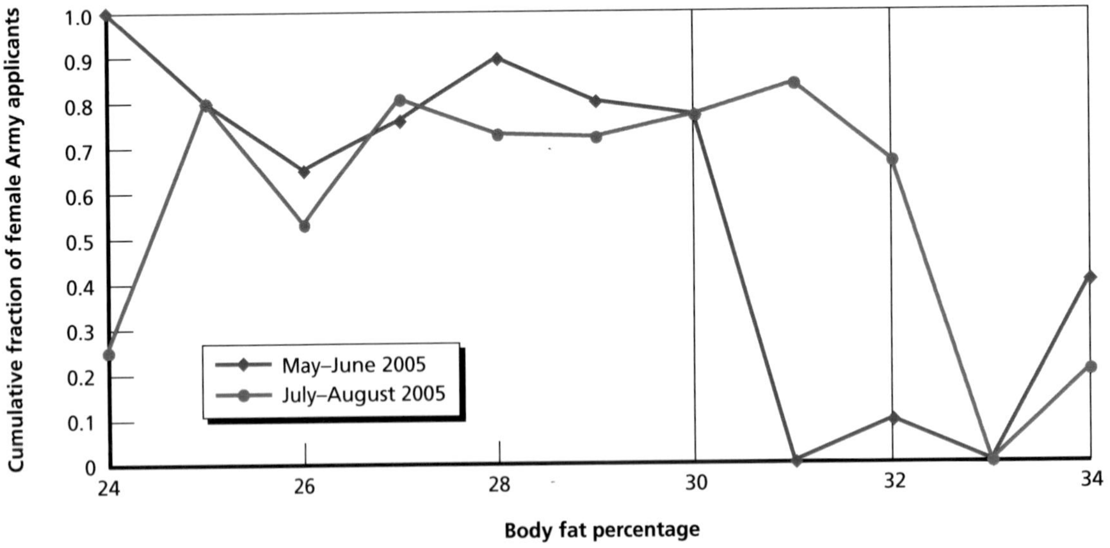

NOTES: The sample is restricted to overweight NPS regular Army female applicants who received their last observed medical exam between May and August 2005. The sample does not include applicants processed by one of the six ARMS study sites. Chapter Two describes additional sample restrictions. Body fat percentage is as recorded at the applicant's last observed medical exam.

RAND *TR975-3.8*

applicants ages 21–27 for whom the official standard (26 and 32, respectively) did not change (see Figures 3.9 and 3.10).

Returning to Figures 3.3 and 3.4, it is also notable that the cumulative distribution of body fat displays a sharp kink at the body fat standard for each gender, indicating an unusually large number of applicants with those specific body fat percentages. In May–June 2005, the cumulative distribution of body fat for applicants ages 17–20 displays a kink at 24 for males and at 30 for females. In July–August 2005, there are kinks at 26 and 32, respectively. For applicants ages 21–27, the kinks occur at 26 and 32 for males and females, respectively, and do not change between May and August 2005. It is a stretch to think that the locations of these kinks at the old and new standards are coincidental. Figures 3.11 (males) and 3.12 (females) show even more clearly that, for an unusually large number of applicants, body fat percentage equaled the body fat standard.

These anomalies in the distribution of body fat percentage among overweight applicants suggest that either recruiters screen applicants in advance so that those who are obviously over–body fat are discouraged from visiting the MEPS until they have lost some weight or there is some manipulation of body fat percentage measurements (or both). In support of the latter hypothesis, we show in Figures 3.13 and 3.14 that there was an unusually large number of applicants whose weight equaled the applicable weight standard (accounting for both age and height). Given how much weight can vary from day to day, these figures suggest some manipulation of weight measurements, which might also suggest manipulation of body fat measurements.

Thus, we believe that at least part of the increase in the body fat percentage of overweight applicants is due to a change in the de facto body fat standard for younger applicants in July 2005. We also believe that some of the increase is due to manipulation of body fat measurements rather than to real changes in the body fat of overweight applicants. Even so, it is important to point out that the mean body fat percentage among younger applicants of both sexes continued to increase in 2006 and, in the case of females, in 2007 as well, even though body fat standards were not changing (see Table 3.1). Moreover, mean body fat percentage increased between 2004 and 2006 among older recruits for whom there was no change in standards, and mean BMI increased between 2004 and 2007 among younger and older recruits alike (see Table 3.2). These trends suggest that at least some of the observed increase in body fat percentage between 2004 and 2007 was in fact real.

There are at least three explanations for why the actual body fat percentage of applicants might have increased between 2004 and 2007, all of which center on the possibility that recruiters became increasingly motivated to pursue overweight applicants. First, following the change in the de facto body fat standards in July 2005, recruiters were now encouraged to bring in younger applicants who would not have met the more-stringent standards. Second, the widespread implementation of ARMS in 2006 encouraged recruiters to bring in applicants of all ages who were over–body fat. Evidence presented in Chapter Four shows that both the weight and body fat percentage of applicants at the ARMS study sites increased between 2004 and 2005 relative to applicants in nonstudy sites. Finally, it could be that the difficult recruiting environment after 2004 caused recruiters to pursue less-qualified applicants. Official Army statistics indicate that the number of NPS Army applicants fell by 8.4 percent between fiscal years (FYs) 2004 and 2007, and our data suggest that the quality of those applicants fell in

Figure 3.9
30-Day Accession Rate, by Body Fat Percentage, in May–August 2005: Overweight Males, Ages 21–27

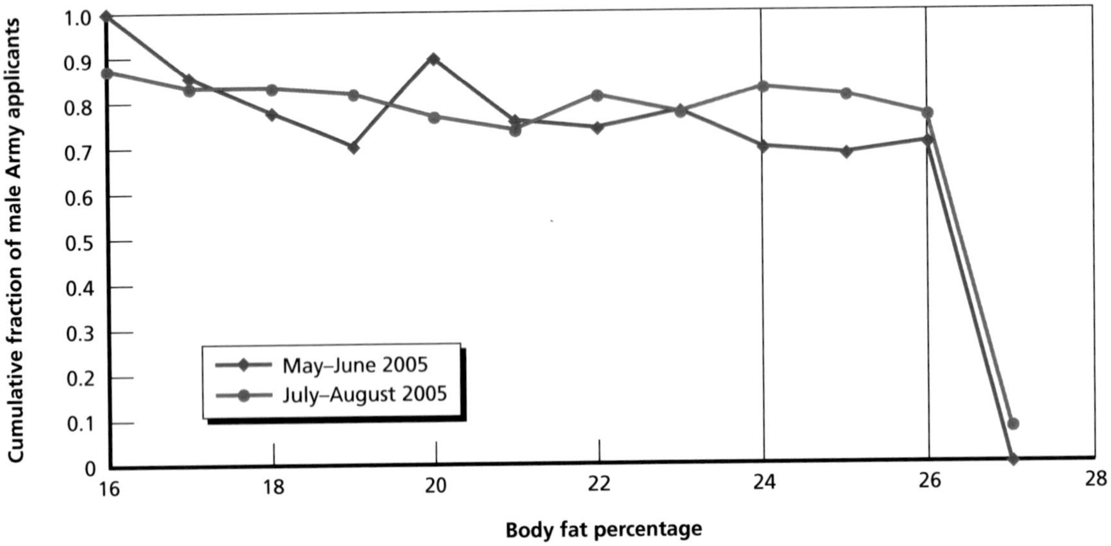

NOTES: The sample is restricted to overweight NPS regular Army male applicants who received their last observed medical exam between May and August 2005. The sample does not include applicants processed by one of the six ARMS study sites. Chapter Two describes additional sample restrictions. Body fat percentage is as recorded at the applicant's last observed medical exam.

RAND *TR975-3.9*

Figure 3.10
30-Day Accession Rate, by Body Fat Percentage, in May–August 2005: Overweight Females, Ages 21–27

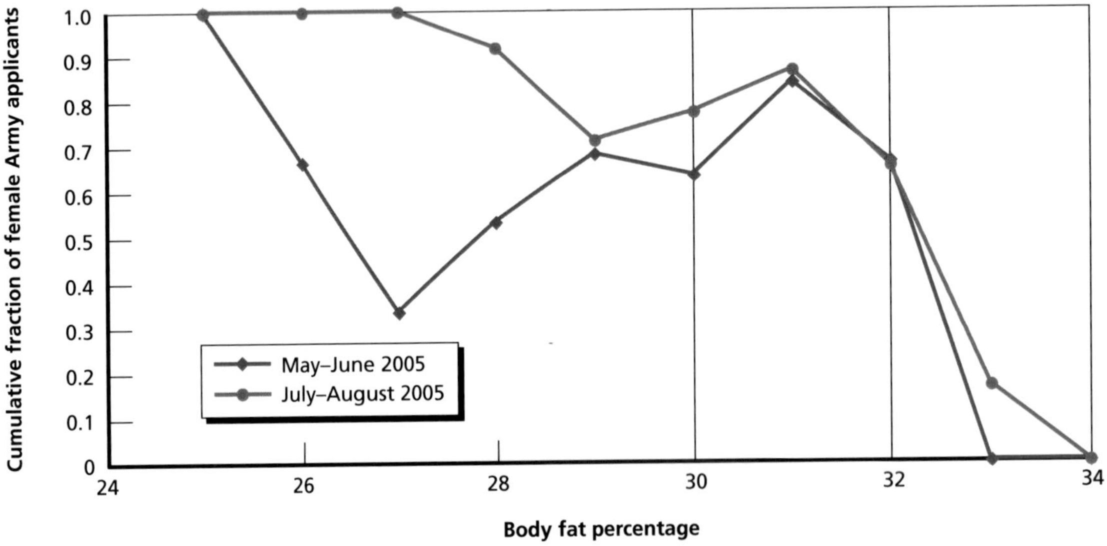

NOTES: The sample is restricted to overweight NPS regular Army female applicants who received their last observed medical exam between May and August 2005. The sample does not include applicants processed by one of the six ARMS study sites. Chapter Two describes additional sample restrictions. Body fat percentage is as recorded at the applicant's last observed medical exam.

RAND *TR975-3.10*

Figure 3.11
Histogram of Body Fat Percentage in 2005: Males, Ages 17–20

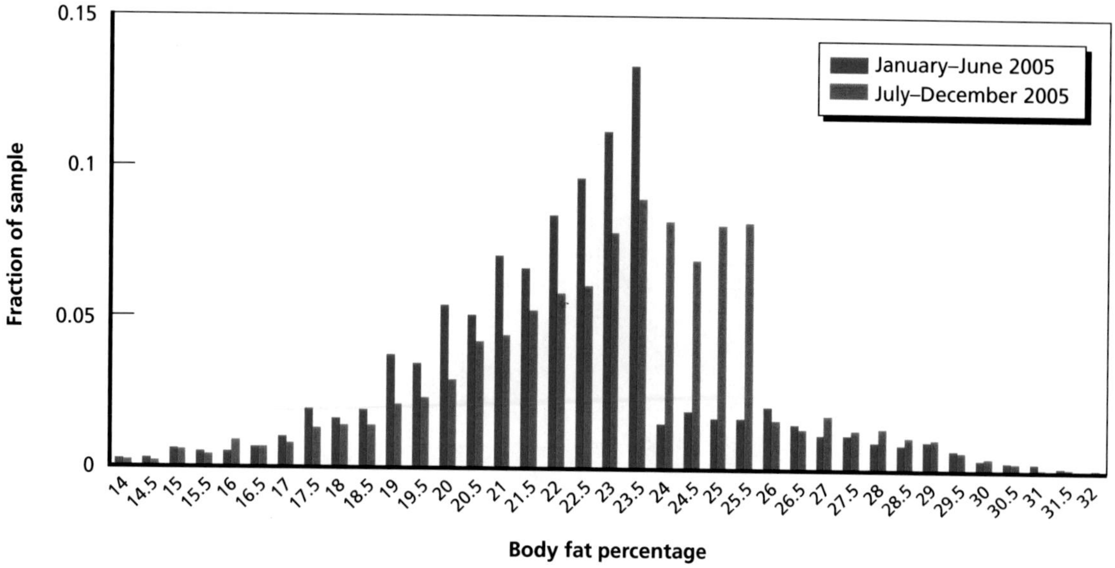

NOTES: The sample is restricted to overweight NPS regular Army male applicants who received their last observed medical exam in 2005. Chapter Two describes additional sample restrictions. Body fat percentage is as recorded at the applicant's last observed medical exam.

RAND *TR975-3.11*

Figure 3.12
Histogram of Body Fat Percentage in 2005: Females, Ages 17–20

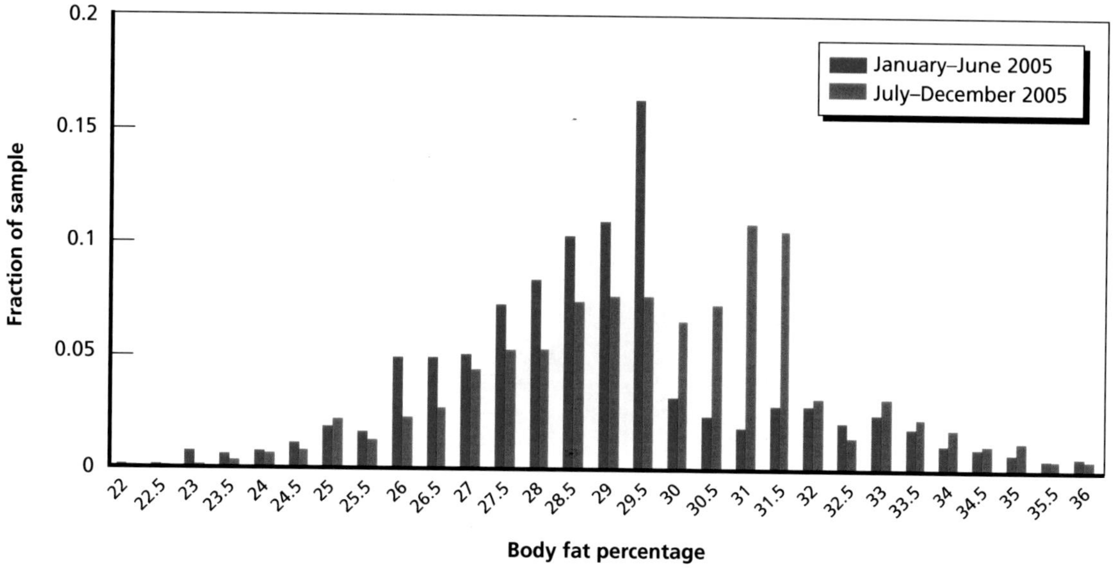

NOTES: The sample is restricted to overweight NPS regular Army female applicants who received their last observed medical exam in 2005. Chapter Two describes additional sample restrictions. Body fat percentage is as recorded at the applicant's last observed medical exam.

RAND *TR975-3.12*

Figure 3.13
Histogram of Weight Relative to the Weight Standard in 2005: Males

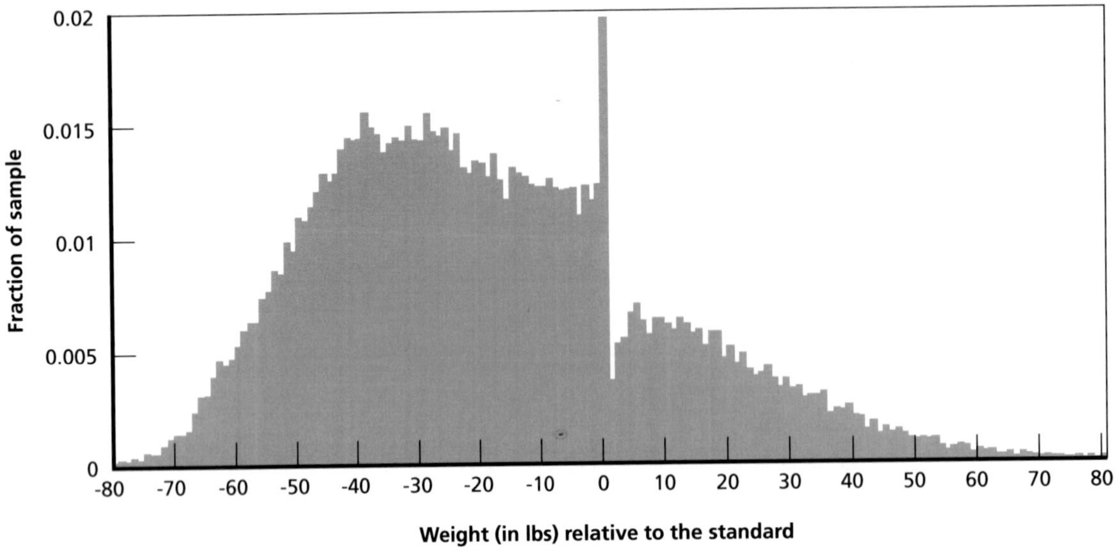

NOTES: The sample is restricted to NPS regular Army male applicants who received their last observed medical exam in 2005. Chapter Two describes additional sample restrictions. Weight and height are as recorded at the applicant's last observed medical exam.

RAND *TR975-3.13*

Figure 3.14
Histogram of Weight Relative to the Weight Standard in 2005: Females

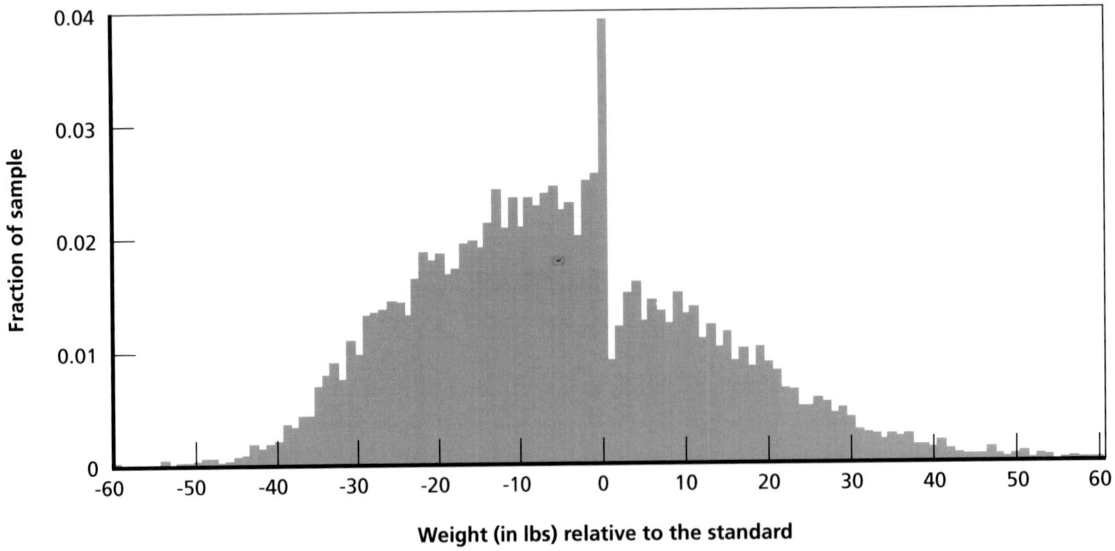

NOTES: The sample is restricted to NPS regular Army female applicants who received their last observed medical exam in 2005. Chapter Two describes additional sample restrictions. Weight and height are as recorded at the applicant's last observed medical exam.

RAND *TR975-3.14*

Table 3.2
Mean BMI of Overweight Applicants, by Gender, Age, and Period

	Period				
Gender and Age	**2004**	**Jan–Jun 2005**	**Jul–Dec 2005**	**2006**	**2007**
A. Males					
17–20	29.7	30.1	30.4	30.7	30.8
21–27	30.2	30.5	30.7	30.9	30.9
28–39	30.8	31.0	31.0	31.0	31.0
B. Females					
17–20	25.5	25.8	26.6	26.6	27.5
21–27	26.4	27.1	27.0	27.2	27.9
28–39	27.6	27.9	28.1	27.9	28.3

NOTES: The sample is restricted to overweight NPS regular Army applicants age 39 or younger who received a medical exam for the first time between January 2004 and September 2007. Chapter Two describes additional sample restrictions. Weight and height are as recorded at the applicant's first medical exam.

other dimensions as well.[3] For example, in our sample, the percentage of recruits scoring at or above the 50th percentile on the AFQT fell from 69 percent to 58 percent between 2004 and 2007.

Whatever the reason, it is clear from the available data that there was a considerable increase in the fraction of applicants eligible for ARMS testing between 2004 and 2007. Had ARMS been implemented in 2004, our data suggest that 1.2 percent of male applicants and 4.1 percent of female applicants would have been eligible for ARMS testing. By 2007, at which time the Army had expanded ARMS to all 65 MEPS, 5.5 percent and 13.1 percent of male and female applicants, respectively, were eligible for ARMS testing.[4]

Characteristics of ARMS Applicants

As explained in Chapter One, implementation of the ARMS program occurred in three phases. In 2005, the Army authorized six MEPS (Atlanta, Buffalo, Chicago, Sacramento, San Antonio, and San Diego) to employ the ARMS test and grant waivers to qualifying overweight or over–body fat applicants. Eight additional MEPS (Beckley, Denver, Jackson, Kansas City, Minneapolis, San Juan, Seattle, and Springfield) were authorized to employ the ARMS test in February 2006. The remaining MEPS implemented ARMS in April 2006. All overweight and over–body fat applicants whose body fat percentage did not exceed maximum limits were

[3] For official statistics on Army NPS applicants in FYs 2004 and 2007, see Table A-1 in Office of the Under Secretary of Defense, Personnel and Readiness, 2006 and undated. Note that part of the decrease is attributable to an offsetting increase in recruiting goals for recruits with prior service.

[4] Note that the percentage of applicants eligible for ARMS testing might have been even higher in 2007 had the Army not relaxed body fat standards for applicants ages 17–20 in July 2006 (or, as we argue above, practically speaking, in July 2005).

eligible to take the ARMS test.[5] In practice, according to our data, 79 percent of eligible applicants took the ARMS test sometime after their first medical exam.[6]

An eligible applicant might not take the ARMS test for any number of reasons. First, the applicant might decide that he or she would rather lose the requisite weight or body fat than be waived in under ARMS. This might be a point of pride, or the applicant might reason that he or she will be in better condition for basic training as a result of losing the weight or body fat. Second, the applicant might face other barriers to enlistment. Third, the applicant might simply decide that he or she is not sufficiently committed to military service to subject himself or herself to the test, even though the time required to take the test is minimal.[7]

There is substantial variation across MEPS in the percentage of eligible applicants who took the ARMS test (see Table A.2): For example, 25 percent of MEPS had ARMS take-up rates of less than 69 percent, and 25 percent of MEPS had ARMS take-up rates of more than 86 percent. Tabulations indicate that the ARMS take-up rate was positively correlated with the fraction of all applicants eligible to take ARMS, the number of pounds overweight and percentage points over–body fat, and the fraction of applicants who were female (the mean male take-up rate was 79 percent, and the mean female take-up rate was 81 percent). All of these factors varied considerably at the MEPS level and can explain a portion of the total variation in take-up rates.[8] For example, 11 percent of Chicago applicants failed to meet the standards, and 94 percent of these applicants took ARMS. In Philadelphia, where the ARMS take-up rate was 66 percent, the fraction failing standards was 6 percent. We also found that the six MEPS study sites and the eight early MEPS had higher ARMS take-up rates than did the remaining MEPS.

Not surprisingly, ARMS applicants were substantially overweight and over–body fat (see Table 3.3). Male ARMS applicants were, on average, 38 pounds overweight (conditional on height and age) and 2.0 percentage points over–body fat. Female applicants were, on average, 27 pounds overweight (conditional on height and age) and 2.1 percentage points over–body fat.

As explained in Chapter One, there are two components of the ARMS test: a step test and a pushup test. The step test is administered first. In Table 3.3, we see that 50 percent of males and 68 percent of females passed the step test. The table further shows that the pushup test was completed by more than 94 percent of applicants who completed the step test; therefore, the overall ARMS pass rate for males and females—48 percent and 65 percent, respectively—was only slightly lower than the step test pass rate.[9] About 15 percent of applicants who failed

---

[5] During the period covered by our data, the maximum body fat limit was 30 percent and 36 percent for males and females, respectively.

[6] The sample we employ here and in the rest of this section is limited to applicants who applied to one of the eight early MEPS between February 2006 and September 2007; to one of the six study sites between October 2006 and September 2007 (the ARMS-specific data we received for these MEPS did not cover the pre–October 2006 period); or to the other MEPS between April 2006 and September 2007.

[7] In conversations with staff at the Pittsburgh, Cleveland, and Los Angeles MEPS, we learned that applicants at those MEPS typically must wait several hours between being told that they are overweight and over–body fat and taking the ARMS test. This delay alone could cause less-committed applicants to suspend their application.

[8] A weighted MEPS-level linear regression of the ARMS take-up rate on the fraction failing standards, mean pounds overweight, mean percent over–body fat, mean male, and whether the MEPS was one of the six study sites or eight early implementers explains 31 percent of the variation in take-up rates.

[9] Taken alone, these data suggest that the pushup test yields little additional information.

Table 3.3
Mean Pounds Overweight, Percentage Points Over–Body Fat, and Proportion Passing ARMS, by Gender

Variable	Males	Females
Pounds overweight	38	27
Percentage points over–body fat	2.0	2.1
Passed step test	0.497	0.680
Passed pushup test and step test	0.958	0.935
Passed ARMS	0.477	0.646
Ever passed ARMS	0.510	0.673
Number of observations	3,008	1,207

NOTES: The sample is restricted to applicants who took the ARMS test between February 2006 and September 2007. The text describes additional sample restrictions. Other than the "Ever passed ARMS" statistics, all statistics correspond to a first ARMS attempt.

ARMS at first returned at a later date to take the test a second time. Thus, the fraction of males (females) who ever passed ARMS was 51 (67) percent.

As with take-up rates, there was substantial variation in ARMS pass rates across MEPS: For example, 25 percent of MEPS had an ARMS pass rate of less than 27 percent, and 25 percent of MEPS had an ARMS pass rate of more than 58 percent (see Table A.2). Some of this variation in ARMS pass rates can be explained by variation in the characteristics of applicants across MEPS. For example, the likelihood of passing ARMS (conditional on taking the test) increases with weight and decreases with body fat.[10] Older recruits (those ages 28–39) were considerably less likely to pass ARMS, and recruits processed by one of the six study sites were considerably more likely to pass ARMS. Race had no effect on pass rates.

Variation in ARMS pass rates across MEPS might also be due to variation in the application of ARMS standards. The step test, for example, requires applicants to maintain a specific cadence, and it is up to an individual MEPS staff member to determine whether that cadence is being met and whether an applicant who falls out of cadence is allowed to resume the test. It seems quite possible that different MEPS personnel maintain different standards, which, assuming that MEPS personnel do not turn over with great frequency, results in systematic variation in pass rates across MEPS.

Table 3.4 suggests that ARMS applicants and non-ARMS applicants differed little along observable dimensions other than in terms of weight and body fat. As expected, ARMS applicants were much heavier than within-standards applicants but, on average, had similar weights and body fat percentages as applicants who exceeded the Army standards but did not take ARMS. The only other notable difference between ARMS and non-ARMS applicants is that ARMS applicants were somewhat less likely, compared with within-standards applicants and over-standards applicants who did not take ARMS, to be African American.

[10] These results are derived from a linear regression of whether an applicant passed the ARMS test on pounds overweight, percentage points over–body fat, gender, and whether the applicant was processed by one of the six study sites or eight early MEPS. It is of some interest that weight and body fat have opposite effects on ARMS pass rates. One possible explanation of this result is that, conditional on body fat, heavier individuals have more lean muscle mass, which is positively correlated with physical fitness (aerobic capacity). Conversely, conditional on weight, individuals with higher body fat have less lean muscle fat, are less physically fit, and so are less likely to pass ARMS.

Table 3.4
Characteristics of Applicants Who Did and Did Not Take the ARMS Test

		Over-Standards Applicants		
Variable	**Within-Standards Applicants**	**Did Not Take ARMS**	**Failed ARMS**	**Passed ARMS**
A. Males				
Age	21.3	20.8	21.3	20.7
Race				
Black	0.205	0.191	0.171	0.207
Other	0.075	0.117	0.077	0.067
AFQT percentile	53.6	51.5	53.6	53.5
Pounds overweight	–9.0	26.4	27.1	27.5
Percentage points over–body fat	–2.5	2.0	2.0	2.2
Number of observations	72,743	860	1,574	1,434
B. Females				
Age	21.2	21.4	21.0	20.7
Race				
Black	0.133	0.114	0.089	0.095
Other	0.053	0.054	0.044	0.051
AFQT percentile	57.4	56.6	57.4	57.4
Pounds overweight	–21.9	35.3	37.4	39.1
Percentage points over–body fat	–3.2	1.9	2.1	2.0
Number of observations	12,301	275	428	779

NOTES: The sample is restricted to NPS regular Army applicants who applied at MEPS that offered the ARMS test between February 2006 and September 2007. Chapter Two describes additional sample restrictions. All variables were measured at the applicant's first medical exam.

CHAPTER FOUR

The Effect of ARMS on Army Accessions

There are at least two ways in which ARMS could increase Army accessions. The most obvious and direct way is by increasing the accession rate: With ARMS, overweight and over–body fat applicants who pass the test and would otherwise have been turned away are now permitted to enlist. But ARMS could also increase accessions by increasing the number of overweight and over–body fat individuals who apply: Some overweight and over–body fat individuals who might otherwise have been discouraged to apply are now encouraged to apply because they can enlist if they pass the test. Thus, ARMS can increase accessions by increasing both the number of applicants and the rate at which those applicants qualify and access.

In this chapter, we present estimates of the effect of ARMS on the number of applicants and accessions processed by individual MEPS and describe the characteristics of those applicants and accessions. We begin by arguing that simply tabulating the number of ARMS applicants who accessed is not likely to yield a reliable estimate of the effect of ARMS on accessions for three reasons. First, many overweight and over–body fat applicants met weight and body fat standards at a later date. Second, some applicants accessed without passing ARMS despite being apparently overweight and over–body fat. Third, ARMS could have had the effect of increasing the number of applicants, not all of whom exceeded weight and body fat standards and therefore required an ARMS waiver. Last, we report statistical estimates of the effect of ARMS on applications and accessions that account for these potential biases.

ARMS Waivers

In principle, ARMS applicants can access in one of two ways. First, if they are overweight and over–body fat at the time of their last physical exam, they can enlist if they have passed the ARMS test. However, if they fail the test, they can, just like any other Army applicant, return at a later date after losing the necessary weight and body fat. As it turns out, a substantial percentage of overweight and over–body fat Army applicants did just that.

Table 4.1 divides Army recruits who did not meet weight and body fat standards at the time of their first physical exam into four groups: (1) non-ARMS applicants applying in 2004 and 2005, (2) non-ARMS applicants applying in February 2006 and later, (3) ARMS applicants who ever passed the ARMS test, and (4) ARMS applicants who never passed the ARMS test. The table, which excludes applicants to one of the six MEPS study sites, shows that, prior to the full implementation of ARMS in 2006, 58 (43) percent of male (female) applicants who failed weight and body fat standards at their first exam returned for a second physical, and 88 (84) percent of those applicants passed weight and body fat standards at that time. Fol-

Table 4.1
Proportion of Overweight and Over–Body Fat Applicants Who Retested and Passed Weight and Body Fat Standards During Their Last Exam, by Gender and ARMS Status

	Retest Rate	Pass Rate[a]	Number of Observations
A. Males			
Non-ARMS, Jan 2004–Dec 2005	0.58	0.88	1,873
Non-ARMS, Feb 2006–Sep 2007	0.48	0.78	1,454
Passed ARMS	0.74	0.26	1,257
Failed ARMS	0.58	0.83	1,325
B. Females			
Non-ARMS, Jan 2004–Dec 2005	0.43	0.84	1,073
Non-ARMS, Feb 2006–Sep 2007	0.38	0.60	625
Passed ARMS	0.68	0.19	710
Failed ARMS	0.55	0.69	359

NOTES: The sample is restricted to overweight NPS regular Army applicants who received a medical exam for the first time between January 2004 and September 2007. Chapter Two describes additional sample restrictions.

[a] Percentage who passed weight and body fat standards during their last exam, conditional on failing standards during their first exam.

lowing implementation of ARMS, these percentages dropped somewhat but remained substantial. Among ARMS applicants who never passed ARMS but received a second physical, 83 (69) percent of male (female) applicants passed weight and body fat standards at a later date. The table also shows that a considerable fraction of ARMS applicants who passed ARMS (26 percent of males and 19 percent of females) passed weight and body fat standards at their last physical exam. Thus, it is clear that, irrespective of ARMS, many overweight and over–body fat applicants eventually lost enough weight and body fat to qualify for enlistment.

The data on ARMS applicants that we obtained from the United States Army Accessions Command do not contain a reliable indicator for whether an ARMS applicant accessed with an actual ARMS waiver. Thus, we can only identify applicants who are likely to have accessed with an ARMS waiver, given that they passed ARMS and failed weight standards at their last physical exam. As Table 4.2 shows, these data indicate that 704 male and 428 female applicants who first applied between February 2006 and June 2007 accessed with an ARMS waiver within 30 days of their last physical exam (recall that our ARMS data exclude applicants who applied at one of the six study sites prior to October 2006).[1] These ARMS accessions represent 47 and 65 percent of male and female ARMS applicants, respectively, during this period, and 1.5 and 5.2 percent of all accessions.

[1] It is likely that these tables underestimate the number of ARMS applicants. The United States Army Accessions Command has estimated that 2,500 regular Army soldiers who enlisted through fiscal year 2010 under the ARMS program were not identified as such due to a data-processing error (email communication with Don Bohn, United States Army Accessions Command February 2, 2010). The data-processing error is related to failure to complete certain date fields, and so it is unlikely that the omission of these recruits from our tables affects the rates we report in this chapter.

Table 4.2
Proportion and Number of Overweight and Over–Body Fat Applicants Who Accessed Within 30 Days of Their Last Physical Exam, by Gender, Whether They Failed Weight and Body Fat Standards at Their Last Exam, and Whether They Took or Ever Passed ARMS

	Failed Weight Standards		Passed Weight Standards	
	Rate of Accession	Number of Accessions	Rate of Accession	Number of Accessions
A. Males				
Non-ARMS, Feb 2006–Jun 2007	0.11	78	0.90	413
Failed ARMS, Feb 2006–Jun 2007	0.04	24	0.94	536
Passed ARMS, Feb 2006–Jun 2007	0.82	704	0.98	226
B. Females				
Non-ARMS, Feb 2006–Jun 2007	0.13	50	0.85	97
Failed ARMS, Feb 2006–Jun 2007	0.08	16	0.92	126
Passed ARMS, Feb 2006–Jun 2007	0.77	428	0.99	83

NOTES: The sample is restricted to NPS regular Army applicants who were overweight and over–body fat at the time of their first medical exam. Chapter Two describes additional sample restrictions.

As Table 4.2 shows, the weighted average of the accession rate among ARMS applicants who passed ARMS and failed weight standards was above 80 percent. The accession rate of applicants who failed weight standards on their first exam but then met weight standards at a later date is very high, between 85 and 99 percent. These high accession rates are perhaps not surprising, since these applicants demonstrated a strong interest in military service by working to lose weight between physical exams.

Difference-in-Differences Estimates

The preceding section suggests several reasons why the count of ARMS applicants who passed ARMS and failed weight standards is not likely to serve as a reasonable estimate of the effect of ARMS on Army accessions. First, before ARMS was implemented, about 45 percent of Army applicants who initially failed weight and body fat standards later met those standards, and 89 percent of those applicants accessed within 30 days of their last physical exam. Second, some Army applicants accessed prior to ARMS even though our records indicate that they were overweight and over–body fat. Our data suggest that about 9 percent of overweight and over–body fat applicants whose last physical exam occurred in 2004 accessed within 30 days of that last exam. To the best of our knowledge, the Army does not permit overweight and over–body fat applicants to access, so these accessions could be the result of data error (e.g., our data fail to record a subsequent physical exam, at which time these accessions met standards) rather than of waivers for weight.

Both of these arguments suggest that a simple count of ARMS applicants who passed ARMS and failed standards could overestimate the effect of ARMS on accessions. On the other hand, however, these counts could significantly understate the true effect of ARMS on accessions if ARMS encouraged a broader segment of individuals to apply for military service—including those who might eventually have met weight or body fat standards (or both)—who otherwise would not have applied.

To capture the full effect of ARMS on accessions, we examined changes in accessions over time in a set of MEPS that did and did not implement ARMS. This difference-in-differences approach assumes that the accession experience of MEPS that did not implement ARMS can serve as the counterfactual experience of MEPS that did implement ARMS (i.e., that the former would have been the experience of the latter had the later not implemented ARMS).

The reader will recall that ARMS waivers were first implemented in six MEPS in February 2005. These six MEPS were the only MEPS authorized to grant ARMS waivers to overweight and over–body fat applicants between February 2005 and January 2006. Thus, our approach was to compare the change in accessions between 2004 and 2005 in the six ARMS study sites with the change in accessions between 2004 and 2005 in the other 59 MEPS.[2] The difference in the change in accession rates between the two groups is an unbiased estimate of the effect of ARMS on accessions, provided that nothing else potentially correlated with accessions, such as local economic conditions, was changing differentially between study and nonstudy sites between 2004 and 2005.[3]

To help explain this approach, it is instructive to construct this difference-in-differences estimate in simple tabular form. In section A of Table 4.3, we see that male accessions occurring within 30 days of the last observed medical exam fell by 11.6 percent between 2004 and 2005 in nonstudy sites but increased by 6.6 percent in study sites.[4] This means that accessions in study sites increased, within rounding, by 6.6 – (–11.6) = 18.3 percent relative to nonstudy sites during that period. Female accessions in study sites increased by 24 percent relative to nonstudy sites. In section B, we see that this relative increase in accessions at study sites was not attributable to a relative increase in the accession rate. In fact, our data indicate that the accession rate in study sites fell relative to nonstudy sites between 2004 and 2005. This suggests that the relative growth in accessions must have been attributable to a relative increase in applications, which is exactly what we see in section C. Male applications at study sites grew by 21 percent relative to nonstudy sites between 2004 and 2005, and female applications grew by 28 percent.

It is notable that the relative growth in both applicants and accessions at ARMS study sites was primarily among overweight applicants and accessions. Male and female overweight but within–body fat applications at the ARMS study sites grew by 21 and 30 percent, respectively, relative to the nonstudy sites between 2004 and 2005 (section E). Male and female over–body fat applications increased by 268 and 197 percent, respectively, relative to the nonstudy sites between 2004 and 2005 (section F). Note also that within-weight applications at ARMS study sites grew relative to nonstudy sites (section D), although by a substantially smaller amount (8.5 and 3.9 percentage points for males and females, respectively) than overweight applica-

---

[2] Throughout this section, we refer to the change in outcomes between 2004 and 2005. More precisely, we mean the change in outcomes between two periods: February 2004–January 2005 and February 2005–January 2006.

[3] A similar approach could be employed using the eight early ARMS sites as the treatment group and the 51 other nonstudy sites as control groups, but the period of analysis would need to be restricted to February and March 2006. This would yield too few observations for meaningful analysis. Moreover, our data suggest that ARMS testing rates were particularly low among the early ARMS sites in those first months of expansion.

[4] All counts are expressed in natural logs. The difference in these log counts approximate percentage changes. Here, the difference rounds to 18.3 percent.

Table 4.3
Change in Application and Accession Outcomes Between 2004 and 2005 Across Study and Nonstudy Sites, by Gender

	Change in Outcome Between 2004 and 2005	
	Males	**Females**
A. Ln(Accessions)		
Nonstudy sites	−0.116	−0.225
Study sites	0.066	0.014
Δ	0.183*	0.239*
B. Accession rate		
Nonstudy sites	−0.012	0.001
Study sites	−0.030	−0.022
Δ	−0.018	−0.023
C. Ln(Applicants)		
Nonstudy sites	−0.100	−0.227
Study sites	0.106	0.048
Δ	0.206*	0.275*
D. Ln(Within-weight applicants)		
Nonstudy sites	−0.107	−0.241
Study sites	−0.021	−0.202
Δ	0.085	0.039
E. Ln(Overweight but within–body fat applicants)		
Nonstudy sites	−0.073	−0.173
Study sites	0.136	0.126
Δ	0.210*	0.300*
F. Ln(Over–body fat applicants)		
Nonstudy sites	−0.010	−0.364
Study sites	2.668	1.603
Δ	2.678*	1.967*
G. Ln(Within-weight accessions)		
Nonstudy sites	−0.116	−0.234
Study sites	−0.045	−0.236
Δ	0.071	−0.002
H. Ln(Overweight but within–body fat accessions)		
Nonstudy sites	−0.121	−0.209
Study sites	0.094	0.138
Δ	0.215*	0.347*

Table 4.3—Continued

	Change in Outcome Between 2004 and 2005	
	Males	**Females**
I. Ln(Over–body fat accessions)		
Nonstudy sites	0.378	0.182
Study sites	4.019	3.226
Δ	3.640*	3.043*
J. Category I-IIIA rate		
Nonstudy sites	−0.081	−0.089
Study sites	−0.078	−0.074
Δ	0.002	0.015
Number of observations	108,862	24,173

NOTES: The sample is restricted to NPS regular Army applicants who received their last observed medical exam between February 2004 and January 2006. Chapter Two describes additional sample restrictions. Category I-IIIA recruits are those scoring at or above the 50th percentile of the Armed Forces Qualification Test distribution.

* The difference is statistically significant at the 1-percent confidence level.

tions. The same pattern is evident when we examine accessions (sections G, H, and I). Finally, section J shows that the strong relative increase in the number of overweight and over–body fat applications at study sites was not correlated with a change in the AFQT: The percentage of Category I-IIIA recruits fell by about 8 percentage points at both the study and nonstudy sites.

The tabular analysis in Table 4.3 shows that, compared with nonstudy sites, ARMS study sites experienced markedly different changes in applications and accessions between 2004 and 2005. The question is whether these difference-in-differences can be interpreted as valid estimates of the causal effect of ARMS. There are at least three concerns with placing a causal interpretation on these difference-in-differences estimates. First, the experience of the study sites might not be representative of the experience of MEPS that adopted ARMS at a later date. Second, difference-in-differences estimates might fail to account for the influence of time-varying characteristics of MEPS that are correlated with being a study site and accessions. Third, the ARMS study sites might have drawn some of their additional applicants from neighboring MEPS. We address each of these concerns in turn.

With respect to the generalizability of these results to MEPS that adopted ARMS after the six study sites, our data indicate that, on average, study and nonstudy sites had similar characteristics in 2004 (e.g., statistically indistinguishable mean BMI, failure rate, AFQT scores, African American representation) prior to implementation of ARMS. But it is possible that the implementation of ARMS at these sites might have been more or less effective during this period than it was when ARMS was expanded to the remaining MEPS in 2006. We have no evidence that this was the case, but a conservative interpretation of the difference-in-differences estimates is that they apply only to the experience of implementing ARMS at the study sites in 2005.

The second concern is that applications and accessions could have increased in study sites relative to nonstudy sites for reasons unrelated to the implementation of ARMS.[5] We are not aware of any other recruiting initiatives under way in the Army during this period that would have differentially affected the ARMS study sites, and recruiting resources as measured by number of recruiters did not change differentially across study and nonstudy sites. The average number of recruiters increased by about 17 percent between 2004 and 2005 in both ARMS and non-ARMS study sites.[6] There also is little evidence that local economic conditions, which can affect the supply of applicants, were changing differentially across study and nonstudy sites. In 2004 and 2005, average unemployment in the counties supplying recruits to ARMS study sites was about one-half of a percentage point higher than in counties supplying recruits to nonstudy sites.[7]

To formally test whether applications and accessions changed differentially between study and nonstudy sites between 2004 and 2005, conditional on recruiting resources and local economic conditions, we estimated the following difference-in-differences model that employs data aggregated to the MEPS level:

$$y_{it} = \beta_1 StudySite_i + \beta_2 Y2005_t + \beta_3 (StudySite_i \times Y2005_t) + \beta_4 X_{it} + \beta_5 Z_{it} + \varepsilon_{it}. \quad (4.1)$$

In this model, y_{it} is the mean value of the dependent variable of interest computed at MEPS i in period t (e.g., ln(accessions)), $StudySite_i$ is a dummy variable equal to one if the MEPS is one of the six study sites, $Y2005_t$ is a dummy variable equal to one if the observation is measured between February 2005 and January 2006 (rather than between February 2004 and January 2005), X_{it} is the average unemployment rate of the counties providing applicants to MEPS i in period t, Z_{it} is the average number of recruiters assigned to MEPS i in period t,[8] and ε_{it} is an idiosyncratic error term. We estimate the regression specification in Equation 4.1 by employing weighted least squares with weights based on the number of applicants contributing to the mean of each observation.

The coefficient β_1 measures whether there are any fixed differences across study and nonstudy sites related to the outcome of interest, and β_2 measures the change in the dependent variable across all study and nonstudy MEPS alike. The coefficient β_3 is the difference-in-differences estimator, which captures whether the dependent variable changed differentially across study and nonstudy sites, controlling for changes in economic conditions and recruiting resources. We can interpret $\hat{\beta}_3$ as an unbiased estimate of the causal effect of ARMS, as long

5 The difference-in-differences method controls for fixed differences between study and nonstudy sites as well as time trends common to both site types. However, the method does not control for time-varying factors that differ across study and nonstudy sites and are potentially correlated with applications and accessions.

6 Data on the number of Army recruiters assigned to a given Army recruiting station were obtained from the United States Army Recruiting Command, as was a cross-walk showing which recruiting stations served which counties in a given month in 2004 and 2005. The number of recruiters serving a given county was computed by summing the number of recruiters contributed by each recruiting station for a given county and then averaging that sum over the year. Weighted averages of these county-level rates were then constructed for each year using the fraction of applicants coming from a given county for a given MEPS as weights.

7 Annual county-level unemployment data for 2004 and 2005 were obtained from the U.S. Department of Labor, Bureau of Labor Statistics (undated). Weighted averages of these county-level rates were constructed for each year using the fraction of applicants coming from a given county for a given MEPS as weights.

8 The two previous footnotes explain how the unemployment and recruiter variables were computed.

as unobserved factors varying across study and nonstudy sites correlated with the implementation of ARMS and as long as our outcomes of interest are fixed over time and so controlled for by the $StudySite_i$ dummy variable. However, if these unobserved factors were trending differentially in study and nonstudy sites and are not captured by the time-varying covariates X_{it} and Z_{it}, the difference-in-differences estimate, $\hat{\beta}_3$, may be biased.

Tables 4.4 and 4.5 report the estimates of the coefficients in Equation 4.1 and their standard errors for the outcomes tabulated in Table 4.3 by gender. The results are consistent with the tabular difference-in-differences estimates reported in Table 4.3. ARMS study sites experienced relative increases in applications and accessions, and those applicants and accessions were disproportionately overweight and over–body fat. The difference-in-differences estimates

Table 4.4
Difference-in-Differences Estimates of the Effect of ARMS on Application and Accession Outcomes: Males

Dependent Variable	*Study Site*$_i$	*Y2005*$_t$	*Study Site*$_i$ · *Y2005*$_t$	X_{it}	Z_{it}
Ln(Accessions)	0.134	−0.164	0.162	−0.019	0.016
	(0.134)	(0.031)	(0.055)	(0.047)	(0.002)
Accession rate	0.015	−0.012	−0.018	0.0004	0.0002
	(0.015)	(0.005)	(0.014)	(0.003)	(0.0001)
Ln(Applicants)	0.115	−0.148	0.184	−0.020	0.016
	(0.135)	(0.029)	(0.045)	(0.046)	(0.002)
Ln(Within-weight applicants)	0.111	−0.157	0.061	−0.024	0.016
	(0.132)	(0.028)	(0.060)	(0.045)	(0.002)
Ln(Overweight but within–body fat applicants)	0.135	−0.109	0.196	0.004	0.015
	(0.182)	(0.040)	(0.046)	(0.052)	(0.002)
Ln(Over–body fat applicants)	−0.020	−0.090	2.621	−0.048	0.016
	(0.158)	(0.086)	(0.179)	(0.073)	(0.003)
Ln(Within-weight accessions)	0.130	−0.167	0.049	−0.026	0.016
	(0.129)	(0.030)	(0.068)	(0.046)	(0.002)
Ln(Overweight but within–body fat accessions)	0.136	−0.154	0.207	0.008	0.015
	(0.193)	(0.043)	(0.066)	(0.052)	(0.002)
Ln(Over–body fat accessions)	−0.462	−0.042	3.914	0.134	0.011
	(0.242)	(0.198)	(0.276)	(0.103)	(0.004)
Category I-IIIA rate	0.005	−0.089	0.003	−0.022	−0.001
	(0.018)	(0.006)	(0.015)	(0.015)	(0.0003)

NOTES: Each row reports the coefficients estimated from the regression specified in Equation 4.1 for the indicated dependent variable. The sample is restricted to NPS regular Army male applicants who received their last observed medical exam between February 2004 and January 2006 (*number of observations* = 108,862). Chapter Two describes additional sample restrictions. Standard errors are in parentheses.

Table 4.5
Difference-in-Differences Estimates of the Effect of ARMS on Application and Accession Outcomes: Females

Dependent Variable	*Study Site$_i$*	*Y2005$_t$*	*Study Site$_i$* · *Y2005$_t$*	X_{it}	Z_{it}
Ln(Accessions)	0.098	−0.299	0.215	−0.040	0.018
	(0.159)	(0.037)	(0.109)	(0.054)	(0.002)
Accession rate	−0.007	0.003	−0.023	0.008	0.001
	(0.039)	(0.010)	(0.029)	(0.005)	(0.0003)
Ln(Applicants)	0.115	−0.304	0.243	−0.051	0.017
	(0.151)	(0.034)	(0.074)	(0.056)	(0.002)
Ln(Within-weight applicants)	0.140	−0.321	−0.003	−0.045	0.019
	(0.156)	(0.036)	(0.077)	(0.057)	(0.002)
Ln(Overweight but within–body fat applicants)	0.020	−0.239	0.279	−0.061	0.013
	(0.184)	(0.041)	(0.121)	(0.057)	(0.002)
Ln(Over–body fat applicants)	0.143	−0.375	1.989	−0.130	0.008
	(0.369)	(0.116)	(0.258)	(0.081)	(0.003)
Ln(Within-weight accessions)	0.141	−0.311	−0.035	−0.038	0.020
	(0.175)	(0.042)	(0.105)	(0.056)	(0.002)
Ln(Overweight but within–body fat accessions)	−0.026	−0.266	0.319	−0.039	0.014
	(0.166)	(0.046)	(0.113)	(0.055)	(0.002)
Ln(Over–body fat accessions)	−0.065	−0.224	2.938	−0.001	0.005
	(0.253)	(0.170)	(0.387)	(0.081)	(0.003)
Category I-IIIA rate	−0.014	−0.096	0.015	−0.019	0.0003
	(0.027)	(0.010)	(0.024)	(0.012)	(0.0003)

NOTES: Each row reports the coefficients estimated from the regression specified in Equation 4.1 for the indicated dependent variable. The sample is restricted to NPS regular Army female applicants who received their last observed medical exam between February 2004 and January 2006 (*number of observations* = 24,173). Chapter Two describes additional sample restrictions. Standard errors are in parentheses.

imply that ARMS increased overweight but within–body fat male and female accessions by 21 and 32 percent, respectively, and over–body fat male and female accessions by 391 and 294 percent, respectively. The effect of ARMS on overweight male (female) accessions overall was 35 (62) percent. These results also indicate that ARMS had no statistically significant effect on within-weight accessions, which bolsters the case for interpreting these difference-in-differences estimates as causal estimates of the true effect of ARMS on accessions, since we would expect ARMS to yield a larger number of overweight accessions but not necessarily a larger number of within-weight accessions. Moreover, we would expect part of the increase in overweight accessions to come from individuals who were not necessarily over–body fat.

Although we have controlled for differences in changes in economic conditions and recruiter supply across study and nonstudy sites,[9] other unobserved differences might remain, and we cannot know whether these differences are correlated with our outcomes of interest. However, we do know that the six study sites as a group represent somewhat larger recruiting markets than do the nonstudy sites. The smallest study site had 723 applicants in 2004, which exceeds the number of applicants in more than 25 percent of the nonstudy sites. Given the possibility that these differences in market size could capture unobservable differences across study and nonstudy sites that are correlated with changes in our outcomes of interest, we exclude the bottom 25 percent of nonstudy sites in terms of number of applicants (i.e., nonstudy sites with fewer than 1,031 applicants) from our analysis. Table 4.6 shows that, across all outcomes, the difference-in-differences results are qualitatively similar to those reported for the full sample in Tables 4.4 and 4.5.

A final concern with these difference-in-differences estimates is that they could overestimate the effect of ARMS if the MEPS study sites in fact drew overweight applicants from nearby MEPS. If this were true, then at least part of the estimated effect of ARMS could be attributable to a redistribution of overweight applicants rather than to an actual increase in their number. For example, an overweight applicant who, in the absence of ARMS, might have applied to the Milwaukee MEPS might, after ARMS, have chosen to apply to the Chicago MEPS study site, knowing that his or her enlistment prospects were better because of ARMS.

We investigated this hypothesis by examining whether the distribution of the home county of overweight applicants to the study-site MEPS locations changed significantly between 2004 and 2005. To do this, we first defined a reference group of counties that accounted for a significant proportion of applicants to a given study site in 2004. As expected, these counties were generally geographically proximate to the study-site MEPS locations. We then determined what fraction of applicants to a given MEPS came from those same reference counties in 2005. If ARMS created incentives for overweight applicants to seek a MEPS that offered ARMS waivers, we would expect to see the fraction of overweight applicants coming from the reference counties fall between 2004 and 2005 relative to the change in the fraction of all applicants coming from those same reference counties.

To make this concrete, consider the first data row of Table 4.7. Between 2004 and 2005, the fraction of applicants coming from counties that accounted for approximately 40 percent of the applicant pool in 2004 fell by about 2 percent. However, the share of overweight applicants coming from those same counties fell by even more—6.8 percent—between 2004 and 2005. We observe the same pattern of results as we increase the share of 2004 applicants accounted for by the reference counties. These tabulations indicate that, between 2004 and 2005, MEPS study sites experienced a significant change in the distribution of their overweight applicants' home counties, which suggests that some overweight applicants who would have applied to a nonstudy site MEPS in 2004 decided to apply to a study-site MEPS in 2005, presumably so that they could qualify for enlistment with an ARMS waiver.

[9] The estimates reported in Tables 4.4 and 4.5 suggest that changes in unemployment were insufficient to affect applications or accessions during the study period but that changes in recruiting resources did have an effect. However, the difference-in-differences estimates are not significantly affected by the inclusion of these covariates in the model.

Table 4.6
Difference-in-Differences Estimates of the Effect of ARMS on Application and Accession Outcomes, Excluding Small Nonstudy Sites

	Study Site$_i$ · Y2005$_t$	
Dependent Variable	**Males**	**Females**
Ln(Accessions)	0.168	0.230
	(0.055)	(0.111)
Accession rate	–0.018	–0.019
	(0.015)	(0.029)
Ln(Applicants)	0.191	0.251
	(0.044)	(0.075)
Ln(Within-weight applicants)	0.069	0.007
	(0.058)	(0.077)
Ln(Overweight but within–body fat applicants)	0.199	0.287
	(0.046)	(0.119)
Ln(Over–body fat applicants)	2.673	1.919
	(0.183)	(0.264)
Ln(Within-weight accessions)	0.057	–0.020
	(0.067)	(0.106)
Ln(Overweight but within–body fat accessions)	0.207	0.332
	(0.065)	(0.112)
Ln(Over–body fat accessions)	3.921	2.951
	(0.287)	(0.393)
Category I-IIIA rate	0.004	0.013
	(0.016)	(0.024)
Number of observations	99,554	22,148

NOTES: Each row reports the difference-in-differences coefficient estimated from the regression specified in Equation 4.1 for the indicated dependent variable. The sample is restricted to NPS regular Army applicants who received their last observed medical exam between February 2004 and January 2006. The sample excludes nonstudy sites with fewer than 1,031 applicants. Chapter Two describes additional sample restrictions. Standard errors are in parentheses.

The results reported in Table 4.7 suggest that the ARMS study sites drew overweight applicants from nearby MEPS locations. To test whether this migration of applicants affects our difference-in-differences estimates, we dropped from our analysis MEPS locations that are geographically proximate to the ARMS study sites and then restricted the applicant pool to applicants who came from the counties accounting for 70 percent of the overweight applicant pool in 2004.[10] The difference-in-differences results accounting for these sample restrictions and presented in Table 4.8 are qualitatively similar to those presented in Tables 4.4–4.6 but somewhat smaller in magnitude and less precisely estimated.[11]

Table 4.7
Share of Overweight and Within-Weight Applicants at Study-Site MEPS in 2005 Accounted for by Counties Representing Various Shares of Overweight and Within-Weight Applicants at Study Site MEPS in 2004

Counties Representing Indicated Share of Applicants in 2004	Change in Share of Applicants Between 2004 and 2005		
	All Applicants	Overweight Applicants	Difference
40%	−0.020	−0.068	0.048
50%	−0.036	−0.089	0.053
60%	−0.053	−0.121	0.068
70%	−0.054	−0.145	0.091
80%	−0.058	−0.155	0.097
90%	−0.064	−0.165	0.100
95%	−0.062	−0.166	0.104
99%	−0.057	−0.143	0.086

NOTES: The sample is restricted to NPS regular Army applicants who received their last observed medical exam between February 2004 and January 2006. The sample is further restricted to applicants who applied to one of the six study sites (*number of observations* = 17,378). Chapter Two describes additional sample restrictions. Weight and height are as recorded at the applicant's first medical exam.

[10] A proximate MEPS is a MEPS location that is within a 300-mile drive of one of the study sites. These non–study site MEPS are the MEPS in Albany, Charlotte, Cincinnati, Cleveland, Dallas, Detroit, Fort Jackson, Harrisburg, Houston, Indianapolis, Knoxville, Lansing, Los Angeles, Louisville, Milwaukee, Montgomery, Nashville, Oakland, Pittsburgh, St. Louis, Syracuse, and Wilkes Barre. We used Google Maps to determine the driving distance between study and non-study sites.

[11] These results are qualitatively similar when we restrict applicants to those coming from counties accounting for 50 percent of the overweight applicant pool and to those coming from counties accounting for 90 percent of the overweight applicant pool.

Table 4.8
Difference-in-Differences Estimates of the Effect of ARMS on Application and Accession Outcomes: Excluding MEPS That Are Geographically Proximate to Study Sites

	Study Site$_i$ · Y2005$_t$	
Dependent Variable	**Males**	**Females**
Ln(Accessions)	0.125	0.198
	(0.085)	(0.119)
Accession rate	–0.021	0.012
	(0.018)	(0.032)
Ln(Applicants)	0.151	0.168
	(0.081)	(0.097)
Ln(Within-weight applicants)	0.070	–0.017
	(0.081)	(0.094)
Ln(Overweight but within–body fat applicants)	0.162	0.194
	(0.097)	(0.158)
Ln(Over–body fat applicants)	2.724	1.498
	(0.245)	(0.434)
Ln(Within-weight accessions)	0.066	0.007
	(0.089)	(0.101)
Ln(Overweight but within–body fat accessions)	0.132	0.256
	(0.107)	(0.166)
Ln(Over–body fat accessions)	3.498	1.915
	(0.228)	(0.651)
Ln(Overweight accessions)	0.354	0.616
	(0.092)	(0.181)
Category I-IIIA rate	–0.006	–0.008
	(0.027)	(0.030)
Number of observations	44,109	10,316

NOTES: Each row reports the difference-in-differences coefficient estimated from the regression specified in Equation 4.1 for the indicated dependent variable. The sample is restricted to NPS regular Army applicants who received their last observed medical exam between February 2004 and January 2006 and who lived in counties accounting for 70 percent of the overweight applicant pool in 2004. The sample excludes Los Angeles, Phoenix, Houston, Dallas, Des Moines, Milwaukee, Indianapolis, Detroit, Lansing, Syracuse, Albany, Harrisburg, Cleveland, Memphis, Montgomery, Nashville, and Knoxville. Chapter Two describes additional sample restrictions. Standard errors are in parentheses.

CHAPTER FIVE

The Effect of ARMS on Attrition

The ARMS test was originally conceived of as an alternative means of screening for the level of physical fitness and motivation necessary to complete basic training. Initial evaluations of the ARMS test in 2004 determined that it was in fact highly predictive of short-run attrition (Niebuhr et al., 2008). However, ARMS was not implemented in 2005 and 2006 as an alternative screening mechanism for the applicant population at large but rather specifically for the population of overweight and over–body fat applicants. Thus, it was hoped that implementation of ARMS would increase accessions of overweight and over–body fat applicants without increasing attrition. The results presented in Chapter Four suggest that, at least at the six study sites, ARMS did succeed in increasing accessions. In this chapter, we examine whether those accessions came at the cost of higher attrition rates. We also examine whether attrition rates varied with differences across MEPS in measures of how ARMS was implemented, including the fraction of over–body fat applicants who took ARMS and the fraction of ARMS applicants who passed the test.

The Effect of Weight and Body Fat on Attrition

We begin by examining how 6- and 18-month attrition rates varied with weight and body fat as measured at the enlistee's first medical exam.[1] Table 5.1 tabulates attrition rates for enlistees whose last medical exam occurred in 2004, prior to the implementation of ARMS at the six study sites in February 2005.[2] For males, the table shows that 6-month attrition rates increased from an average of 12.0 percent for within-weight male enlistees to

- 14.7 percent for male enlistees who were 1–15 pounds overweight but were within body fat standards
- 16.4 percent for male enlistees who were more than 15 pounds overweight but were within body fat standards
- 20.9 percent for male enlistees who accessed while over–body fat.

1 These results remain substantively unchanged if we categorize applicants according to their weight and body fat at the time of their last physical exam.

2 Throughout this chapter, we restrict our sample to applicants who accessed within 30 days of their last observed medical exam.

Table 5.1
Attrition Rates, by Gender and Weight and Body Fat Percentage Relative to Army Standards: FY 2004

Weight and Body Fat Relative to Army Standards	Males			Females		
	6-Month Attrition Rate	18-Month Attrition Rate	*Number of Observations*	6-Month Attrition Rate	18-Month Attrition Rate	*Number of Observations*
Within-weight	0.120	0.189	34,914	0.222	0.347	6,515
1–15 lbs overweight, within–body fat	0.147*	0.215*	4,169	0.225	0.357	1,853
>15 lbs overweight, within–body fat	0.164*	0.227*	3,947	0.232	0.358	671
>0 lbs overweight, not within–body fat	0.209*	0.266*	139	0.210	0.371	62

NOTES: The sample is restricted to NPS regular Army enlistees who received their last observed medical exam between January and December 2004 and accessed within 30 days of that exam. Chapter Two describes additional sample restrictions. Weight and body fat are as recorded at the applicant's first medical exam.

* Statistically different from the attrition rate of within-weight enlistees at the 1-percent confidence level.

A similar pattern is evident in 18-month male attrition rates. Attrition rates for overweight and over–body fat female enlistees were not significantly different from those of within-weight enlistees.

In Table 5.2, our sample is enlistees whose last medical exam occurred between October 2006 and September 2007, including enlistees who took the ARMS test. As in Table 5.1, we see that attrition rates were elevated among overweight but within–body fat male enlistees. We also see that attrition rates were even higher among over–body fat male enlistees who either failed or did not take the ARMS test but that attrition rates among over–body fat male enlistees who passed the ARMS test were no higher than those of within-weight enlistees. These data suggest that the ARMS test is effective at identifying over–body male fat applicants who are as likely to complete initial training as within-weight male applicants. Female enlistees who failed ARMS also had elevated attrition rates relative to within-weight enlistees. Female enlistees who passed ARMS had somewhat lower 18-month attrition rates than did within-weight female enlistees.

In Table 5.3, we examine how the characteristics of ARMS enlistees and the MEPS to which they applied affected six-month attrition rates. We do this by estimating an individual-level linear probability regression of six-month attrition on a host of individual-level characteristics, such as BMI, body fat, pulse before taking the ARMS test,[3] whether the enlistee failed body fat standards at his or her last physical exam, whether the enlistee passed the ARMS test on his or her first attempt, the number of ARMS attempts made by the enlistee, and the enlistee's AFQT score, race, age, and month of application. We also included in these regressions the number of applicants applying to the enlistee's MEPS and the fraction of over–body fat applicants who took ARMS at that MEPS (computed by gender). We restrict the sample to enlistees who took the ARMS test in FY 2007 and who accessed prior to November 2007. The regressions are estimated separately by gender, and standard errors are clustered at the MEPS level.

[3] We could have included the post-test pulse rate as well, but interpreting the estimated effect of that variable in this regression is complicated by the fact that a substantial fraction of individuals who do not pass the test give up soon after starting the test; the pulse rate for these individuals could be low despite the individuals' low level of physical fitness.

Table 5.2
Attrition Rates, by Gender and Weight and Body Fat Percentage Relative to Army Standards: FY 2007

Weight and Body Fat Relative to Army Standards	Males			Females		
	6-Month Attrition Rate	18-Month Attrition Rate	*Number of Observations*	6-Month Attrition Rate	18-Month Attrition Rate	*Number of Observations*
Within-weight	0.055	0.145	55,635	0.104	0.294	8,201
1–15 lbs overweight, within–body fat	0.060	0.144	5,703	0.102	0.278	1,598
>15 lbs overweight, within–body fat	0.075*	0.159*	6,731	0.113	0.292	1,108
>0 lbs overweight, not within–body fat, no ARMS test	0.080*	0.169**	1,129	0.083	0.261	399
Failed ARMS	0.090*	0.180*	645	0.155**	0.361***	155
Passed ARMS	0.064	0.141	1,251	0.092	0.256**	644

NOTES: The sample is restricted to NPS regular Army enlistees who received their last observed medical exam between October 2006 and September 2007 and accessed within 30 days of that exam. Chapter Two describes additional sample restrictions. Weight and body fat are as recorded at the applicant's first medical exam.

* Statistically different from the attrition rate of within-weight enlistees at the 1-percent confidence level.

** Statistically different from the attrition rate of within-weight enlistees at the 5-percent confidence level.

*** Statistically different from the attrition rate of within-weight enlistees at the 10-percent confidence level.

Table 5.3
The Effect of Individual-Level and MEPS-Level Characteristics on Six-Month Attrition: Enlistees Who Took ARMS in FY 2007

	Males	Females
BMI	0.005	0.012
	(0.003)***	(0.010)
Body fat percentage	−0.001	−0.004
	(0.005)	(0.010)
Failed weight standard	0.018	0.035
	(0.015)	(0.025)
Passed ARMS	−0.054	−0.045
	(0.018)*	(0.032)
Number of ARMS tests	−0.001	−0.034
	(0.025)	(0.029)
Pulse before	0.001	0.001
	(0.001)	(0.001)***
AFQT percentile	−0.001	−0.001
	(0.0003)**	(0.001)

Table 5.3—Continued

	Males	Females
Race/ethnicity		
Black	−0.008	−0.006
	(0.019)	(0.037)
Nonblack, nonwhite	0.004	−0.015
	(0.032)	(0.065)
Race unknown	0.017	−0.019
	(0.023)	(0.046)
Age	0.001	−0.006
	(0.002)	(0.003)**
MEPS characteristics		
Percentage eligible to take ARMS	0.142	−0.022
	(0.074)***	(0.126)
Number of applicants	0.000002	−0.0002
	(0.00001)	(0.0002)
Constant	−0.198	0.087
	(0.185)	(0.395)
Number of observations	1,546	576
R^2	0.02	0.04

NOTES: The dependent variable is whether the enlistee separated within six months of accession. The regression also controls for month of application. The sample is restricted to NPS regular Army enlistees who received their last observed medical exam between October 2006 and September 2007 and accessed within 30 days of that exam. Chapter Two describes additional sample restrictions. BMI and body fat are as recorded at the applicant's first medical exam. Standard errors are clustered at the MEPS level and reported in parentheses.

* Statistically significant at the 1-percent confidence level.

** Statistically significant at the 5-percent confidence level.

*** Statistically significant at the 10-percent confidence level.

For males, and consistent with the tabulations reported in Table 5.2, the regression results reported in Table 5.3 show that over–body fat enlistees who passed the ARMS test were more than 5 percentage points less likely to separate within six months of accession than were overweight enlistees who failed the ARMS test but accessed nonetheless. The regression results also suggest that female enlistees who passed ARMS were less likely to separate than those who failed ARMS, but this correlation is not statistically significant. For male ARMS enlistees, the regression results indicate that loss rates increased with BMI, decreased with AFQT percentile, and increased with the percentage of eligible enlistees who took ARMS at a given MEPS. This last result is consistent with the possibility that MEPS with low ARMS take-up rates, either because their medical staff or the enlistees themselves were more discriminating, accessed a relatively more physically fit group of ARMS enlistees.

Table 5.4 reports the results of a comparable regression in which the sample is restricted to enlistees who likely accessed with an ARMS waiver (i.e., passed the ARMS test and failed weight standards at the time of accession). These results suggest that, among male ARMS accessions, BMI and body fat percentage were not predictive of six-month attrition, presumably because the ARMS test was effective in screening, but that the attrition rate decreased with the enlistee's pulse rate after he took the ARMS test.[4] The regression results suggest that attrition rates among ARMS accessions increased with the fraction of enlistees who took ARMS at a given MEPS and with the fraction who passed ARMS at a given MEPS. This latter result could indicate that MEPS locations that were more permissive in the administration of ARMS accessed male ARMS enlistees who were, on average, less physically qualified. For female ARMS enlistees, the results indicate that the enlistee's pulse rate after taking the

Table 5.4
Effect of Individual-Level and MEPS-Level Characteristics on 6-Month Attrition: Enlistees Likely Accessing with ARMS Waiver, FY 2007

	Males	Females
BMI	0.005	0.009
	(0.004)	(0.012)
Body fat percentage	0.005	–0.007
	(0.008)	(0.013)
Number of ARMS tests	0.010	–0.011
	(0.027)	(0.029)
Pulse before	0.002	0.001
	(0.001)	(0.001)
Pulse after	–0.001	0.001
	(0.0003)*	(0.001)**
Number of pushups	–0.0006	–0.002
	(0.001)	(0.003)
AFQT percentile	–0.001	–0.001
	(0.0004)**	(0.001)***
Race/ethnicity		
Black	–0.033	–0.062
	(0.026)	(0.043)
Nonblack, nonwhite	0.033	–0.017
	(0.048)	(0.087)
Race unknown	0.032	–0.009
	(0.031)	(0.056)

4 The estimated negative correlation between pulse rate and attrition among males is counterintuitive. This correlation is positive among females.

Table 5.4—Continued

	Males	Females
Age	0.003	−0.005
	(0.002)	(0.004)
MEPS characteristics		
Percentage eligible to take ARMS	0.169	−0.115
	(0.088)***	(0.176)
Percentage who passed ARMS	0.095	0.138
	(0.043)**	(0.113)
Number of applicants	−0.000007	−0.0002
	(0.00002)	(0.0002)
Constant	−0.360	0.074
	(0.230)	(0.428)
Number of observations	707	361
R^2	0.05	0.08

NOTES: The dependent variable is whether the enlistee separated within six months of accession. The regression also controls for month of application. The sample is restricted to NPS regular Army applicants who received their last observed medical exam between October 2006 and September 2007, accessed within 30 days of that exam, passed ARMS, and failed weight standards at their last physical exam. Chapter Two describes additional sample restrictions. BMI and body fat are as recorded at the applicant's first medical exam. Standard errors are clustered at the MEPS level and reported in parentheses.

* Statistically significant at the 1-percent confidence level.

** Statistically significant at the 5-percent confidence level.

*** Statistically significant at the 10-percent confidence level.

ARMS test was positively correlated with attrition. MEPS-level characteristics are statistically uncorrelated with attrition among female ARMS enlistees.

Difference-in-Differences Estimates of the Effect of ARMS on Attrition

Although it would appear that overweight male enlistees who passed ARMS had relatively low attrition rates, it is not clear that ARMS resulted in lower attrition rates overall. We know from the results presented in Chapter Four that accessions increased in study sites relative to nonstudy sites and that those accessions were disproportionately overweight and over–body fat. The net effect on attrition rates of this change in the composition of accessions is unclear. On the one hand, attrition was higher among overweight male accessions, which would tend to increase attrition rates under the ARMS program. On the other hand, attrition was lower among overweight accessions who passed the ARMS test. Thus, to the extent that ARMS screens out applicants who might otherwise have accessed and separated, ARMS could result in lower overall attrition rates.

To test whether ARMS affected overall attrition at the six study sites, we employed the same difference-in-differences framework described in Chapter Four, where the dependent variables are mean 6-month and 18-month attrition rates at the MEPS level.[5] The difference-in-differences estimates presented in Tables 5.5 and 5.6 suggest that ARMS had no net effect on male or female attrition rates either in the overall accessions population or in the population of overweight accessions. The estimated coefficient on the interaction between $StudySite_i$ and $Y2005_t$ is small and statistically insignificant for males. For females, the difference-in-differences estimate is positive but statistically insignificant. These null difference-in-differences results are consistent with the possibility that whatever effect ARMS had on elevating attrition rates by increasing the number of overweight but within–body fat accessions was counteracted by the effectiveness of ARMS in identifying overweight and over–body fat applicants likely to complete initial training who otherwise would not have accessed.

Reason for Separation

Although we find that ARMS had no effect on attrition rates, it is nonetheless possible that ARMS accessions who did separate did so for different reasons than their non-ARMS counterparts. In particular, it might be the case that ARMS accessions were more susceptible to injury than their non-ARMS counterparts and were therefore more likely to separate for medical reasons. Table 5.7 tabulates reasons for separation by gender and accession category: (1) within-weight, (2) overweight but within–body fat, (3) over–body fat and not tested under the ARMS program, (4) over–body fat and failed ARMS, and (5) over–body fat and passed ARMS. These tabulations suggest that male accessions who passed the ARMS test and separated within 18 months of accession were somewhat less likely to separate for medical reasons but somewhat more likely than within-weight accessions to separate because they did not meet physical (e.g., weight and body fat) standards. Curiously, the same was true of male accessions who failed the ARMS test and so presumably met weight standards prior to accession. Female accessions who took the ARMS test prior to accession were also less likely than within-weight accessions to separate for medical reasons. This evidence, then, suggests that, if anything, ARMS accessions were less susceptible than non-ARMS accessions to injury that results in separation. (ARMS accessions also appear to have been no more likely than within-weight accessions to separate for conduct-related or other reasons.) However, it might still be the case that ARMS accessions were more likely than non-ARMS accessions to suffer injury that impedes performance but does not result in separation. We did not have access to data that would allow us to investigate this issue.

---

[5] Unlike Tables 4.6 and 4.8, Tables 5.5 and 5.6 report regressions that do not exclude smaller MEPS or geographically proximate nonstudy-site MEPS. Employing these sample restrictions yields qualitatively similar results.

Table 5.5
Difference-in-Differences Estimates of the Effect of ARMS on 6- and 18-Month Attrition Rates: Males

Dependent Variable	*Study Site*$_i$	*Y2005*$_t$	*Study Site*$_i$ · *Y2005*$_t$	X_{it}	Z_{it}
A. 6-month attrition rate					
Overall	−0.003	−0.064	−0.004	−0.002	−0.0002
	(0.010)	(0.002)	(0.008)	(0.002)	(0.00006)
Overweight	−0.020	−0.087	0.017	−0.003	−0.0002
	(0.018)	(0.006)	(0.017)	(0.003)	(0.00009)
B. 18-month attrition rate					
Overall	−0.008	−0.053	0.007	−0.005	−0.0005
	(0.011)	(0.003)	(0.010)	(0.002)	(0.0001)
Overweight	−0.012	−0.078	0.026	−0.005	−0.0005
	(0.018)	(0.008)	(0.017)	(0.004)	(0.0001)

NOTES: Each row reports the coefficients estimated from the regression specified in Equation 4.1 for the indicated dependent variable. The sample is restricted to NPS regular Army male enlistees who received their last observed medical exam between February 2004 and January 2006 and accessed within 30 days of that exam (*number of observations* = 82,153). Chapter Two describes additional sample restrictions. Standard errors are in parentheses.

Table 5.6
Difference-in-Differences Estimates of the Effect of ARMS on 6-and 18-Month Attrition Rates: Females

Dependent Variable	*Study Site*$_i$	*Y2005*$_t$	*Study Site*$_i$ · *Y2005*$_t$	X_{it}	Z_{it}
A. 6-month attrition rate					
Overall	−0.010	−0.105	0.028	−0.002	−0.0008
	(0.014)	(0.007)	(0.018)	(0.004)	(0.0001)
Overweight	0.020	−0.092	0.004	0.002	−0.001
	(0.018)	(0.013)	(0.025)	(0.005)	(0.0002)
B. 18-month attrition rate					
Overall	−0.016	−0.062	0.036	−0.003	−0.001
	(0.020)	(0.009)	(0.020)	(0.005)	(0.0002)
Overweight	−0.016	−0.045	0.025	0.003	−0.001
	(0.024)	(0.017)	(0.023)	(0.006)	(0.0003)

NOTES: Each row reports the coefficients estimated from the regression specified in Equation 4.1 for the indicated dependent variable. The sample is restricted to NPS regular Army female enlistees who received their last observed medical exam between February 2004 and January 2006 and accessed within 30 days of that exam (*number of observations* = 16,057). Chapter Two describes additional sample restrictions. Standard errors are in parentheses.

Table 5.7
Reason for Separation, by Gender and Weight and Body Fat Percentage Relative to Army Standards: FY 2007

	Reason for Separation				
Accession Category	**Medical**	**Physical Standards**	**Conduct**	**Other**	***Number of Observations***
A. Males					
Within-weight	0.210	0.174	0.507	0.098	8,066
Overweight, within–body fat	0.232*	0.217*	0.422*	0.107	1,893
Over–body fat, no ARMS test	0.236	0.267*	0.393*	0.105	191
Failed ARMS	0.147*	0.259*	0.457	0.112	116
Passed ARMS	0.182	0.244*	0.432*	0.119	176
B. Females					
Within-weight	0.236	0.174	0.276	0.295	2,410
Overweight, within–body fat	0.243	0.189	0.287	0.280	767
Over–body fat, no ARMS test	0.346*	0.154	0.183*	0.308	104
Failed ARMS	0.107*	0.143	0.429*	0.304	56
Passed ARMS	0.164*	0.188	0.291	0.345	165

NOTES: The sample is restricted to NPS regular Army enlistees who received their last observed medical exam between October 2006 and September 2007, accessed within 30 days of that exam, and separated within 18 months of accession. Chapter Two describes additional sample restrictions. Weight and body fat are as recorded at the applicant's first medical exam.

* The difference from the within-weight mean is statistically significant at the 5-percent confidence level.

CHAPTER SIX
Conclusion

The ARMS test was designed to serve as an indicator for whether a recruit possesses the motivational and physical wherewithal to complete basic training, and early studies indicated that in fact it served that purpose in the overall applicant population. When the Army implemented ARMS at the six study sites in 2005 and then at all MEPS in 2006, the hope was the test would increase accessions among overweight and over–body fat applicants without adversely affecting attrition. The evidence reported here suggests that implementation of ARMS at the six study sites succeeded in doing just that. Our difference-in-differences estimates imply that the implementation of ARMS increased male accessions by 13 percent and female accessions by 20 percent in 2005 (Table 4.8) and that virtually all of that percentage increase came from overweight and over–body fat accessions. Despite the fact that ARMS resulted in a large increase in the proportion of applicants who were overweight and over–body fat, our estimates imply that ARMS had no effect on attrition rates. This suggests that the ARMS test is effective in identifying overweight and over–body fat recruits who are as likely as within-standards recruits to complete basic training. We cannot say for certain whether the broader implementation of ARMS since 2005 has been as successful, but we have no reason to think otherwise. At a minimum, the available evidence indicates that overweight and over–body fat applicants who pass ARMS are no more likely to separate than are applicants who meet those standards.

The Resource Management Directorate within the Office of the Secretary of Defense estimates that the total FY 2007 training, travel, equipment, and personnel costs of ARMS were a little more than $600,000. If we assume that ARMS increased the number of overweight accessions by the same percentage in FY 2007 as our estimates imply it did in 2005 (35 and 62 percent for males and females, respectively), then we would credit ARMS with accessing an additional 3,690 recruits in FY 2007.[1] Dividing ARMS costs by these additional recruits yields a per-recruit cost of $163 in FY 2007.[2]

[1] Official Army statistics show 52,660 (10,236) NPS male (female) accessions in FY 2007 (Office of the Under Secretary of Defense, Personnel and Readiness, undated, Table B.1). Data used in this report suggest that about 21 (24) percent of those male (female) accessions were overweight. If we assume that ARMS increased the number of male (female) overweight accessions by 35 (62) percent and had no effect on the number of within-weight accessions, then these computations imply that ARMS increased FY 2007 male (female) accessions by 2,867 (823).

[2] These costs may over- or underestimate the true costs of ARMS for a number of reasons. On the one hand, the Army National Guard and Reserve presumably benefit from ARMS as well, and those benefits are not included in our estimates. It is also possible that ARMS increased the number of within-weight accessions. On the other hand, because our estimates imply that ARMS increased accessions by increasing applications, the true cost of ARMS should include both the direct costs of administering the ARMS test to eligible applicants and all of the other costs associated with processing additional applicants. Of course, this same caveat applies to cost-benefit analyses of other recruiting resources.

Thus, it appears that ARMS increases accessions at very low cost. But, even more important is that it does so without affecting AFQT scores or attrition. The AFQT distributions of ARMS and within-standard accessions are practically identical (see Figures 6.1 and 6.2), and the estimates reported in Chapter Five suggest that ARMS accessions were no more likely than within-standard accessions to separate. Thus, at least by these short-run measures, ARMS appears to offer a highly cost-effective means of increasing accessions.

However, it remains to be seen whether ARMS accessions in the longer run will turn out to be as productive, on average, as within-standards accessions. Although our tabulations suggest that ARMS accessions were, if anything, somewhat less likely than non-ARMS accessions to separate for medical reasons, Bedno et al. (2010a) find that over–body fat recruits waived in under ARMS were considerably more likely to suffer heat-related illnesses during basic training.[3] Injuries of this sort, while perhaps not resulting in separation, could result in a less-fit and less-productive enlisted force. Moreover, it is important to acknowledge that ARMS appears to have had a strong effect on the number of overweight but within–body fat accessions. These individuals would not be subject to the ARMS test. To the extent that these accessions are more likely to separate than within-weight accessions (which the results of Chapter Five suggest is the case for males), the overall effect of ARMS could be to raise attrition. This caveat is tempered by the finding in Chapter Five that the overall attrition rate at study sites did not change relative to nonstudy sites despite a significant relative change in the number of overweight but within–body fat accessions.

The decision to implement ARMS was made in a weak recruiting environment. Today, the recruiting environment is much stronger (largely because of the weak civilian labor market). However, even in a very strong recruiting environment like the current one, ARMS can serve a highly useful role by identifying enlistees who, despite weight problems, can be productive members of the Army enlisted force. The success of the ARMS test suggests what might appear obvious in hindsight: The population of overweight and over–body fat individuals is quite heterogeneous. Some of these individuals are truly unfit for service, but many others possess the desire and ability to serve their country in the armed forces and, given the chance, will succeed in that capacity. In both weak and strong recruiting environments, then, the ARMS test offers a simple, cost-effective way to separate the fit from the unfit.

---

[3] Bedno et al. (2010b) also find that ARMS recruits are more likely to enroll in the Army Weight Control program. Forthcoming research by Niebuhr and colleagues at the Water Reed Army Institute of Research suggests that ARMS recruits use health care services at a higher rate and have a greater risk of sprains, strains, and other injuries to the back, lower leg, foot, and ankle (communication with David Niebuhr, September 27, 2010).

Figure 6.1
Cumulative Distribution of AFQT Scores, by Whether the Enlistees Accessed Under the ARMS Program: Males

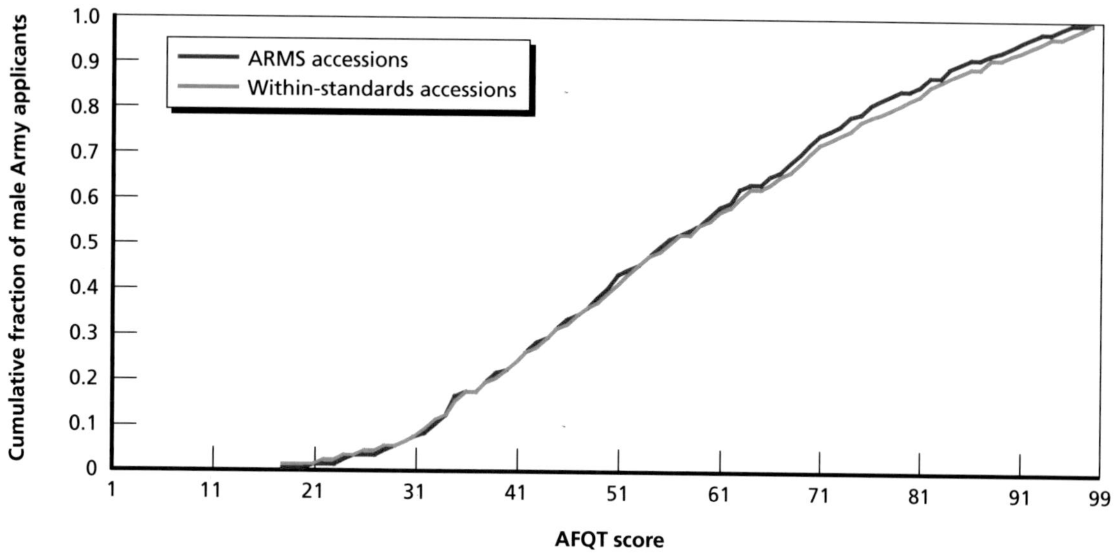

NOTES: The sample is restricted to NPS regular Army male applicants who received their last observed medical exam in FY 2007 and accessed within six months of that exam. Chapter Two describes additional sample restrictions.
RAND *TR975-6.1*

Figure 6.2
Cumulative Distribution of AFQT Scores, by Whether the Enlistees Accessed Under the ARMS Program: Females

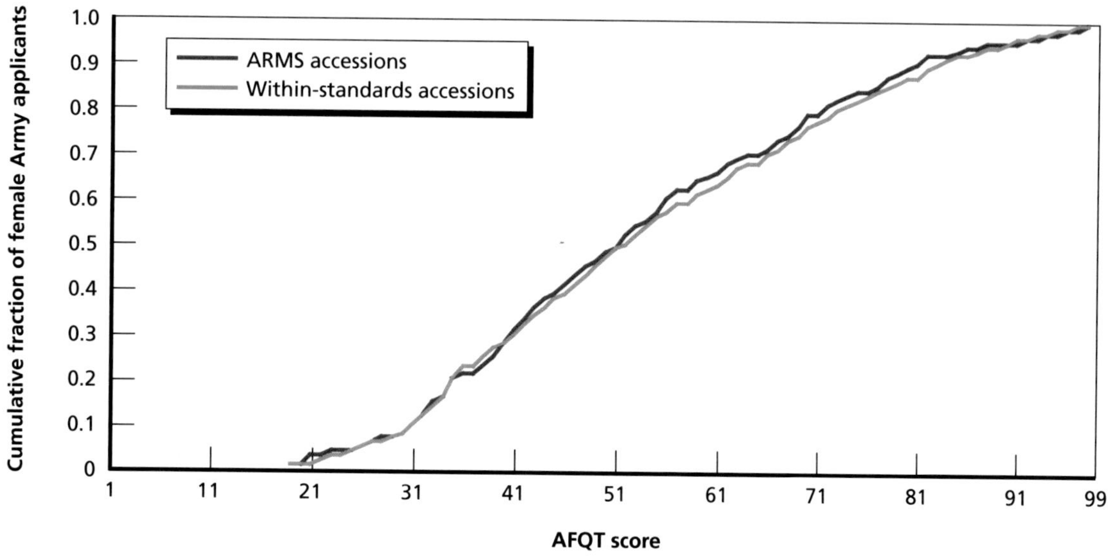

NOTES: The sample is restricted to NPS regular Army female applicants who received their last observed medical exam in FY 2007 and accessed within six months of that exam. Chapter Two describes additional sample restrictions.
RAND *TR975-6.2*

APPENDIX

Additional Tables

Table A.1
Maximum Permitted Weight and Body Fat for NPS Army Enlistees, by Height and Gender

	Ages 17–20		Ages 21–27		Ages 28–39		Age 40 and Over	
Height (inches)	Weight	Body Fat	Weight	Body Fat	Weight	Body Fat	Weight	Body Fat
A. Males								
60	139	26	141	26	143	28	146	30
61	144	26	146	26	148	28	151	30
62	148	26	150	26	153	28	156	30
63	153	26	155	26	158	28	161	30
64	158	26	160	26	163	28	166	30
65	163	26	165	26	168	28	171	30
66	168	26	170	26	173	28	177	30
67	174	26	176	26	179	28	182	30
68	179	26	181	26	184	28	187	30
69	184	26	186	26	189	28	193	30
70	189	26	192	26	195	28	199	30
71	194	26	197	26	201	28	204	30
72	200	26	203	26	206	28	210	30
73	205	26	208	26	212	28	216	30
74	211	26	214	26	218	28	222	30
75	217	26	220	26	224	28	228	30
76	223	26	226	26	230	28	234	30
77	229	26	232	26	236	28	240	30
78	235	26	238	26	242	28	247	30
79	241	26	244	26	248	28	253	30
80	247	26	250	26	255	28	259	30

Table A.1—Continued

	Ages 17–20		Ages 21–27		Ages 28–39		Age 40 and Over	
Height (inches)	Weight	Body Fat	Weight	Body Fat	Weight	Body Fat	Weight	Body Fat
B. Females								
58	112	32	115	32	119	34	122	36
59	116	32	119	32	123	34	126	36
60	120	32	123	32	127	34	130	36
61	124	32	127	32	131	34	135	36
62	129	32	132	32	137	34	139	36
63	133	32	137	32	141	34	144	36
64	137	32	141	32	145	34	148	36
65	141	32	145	32	149	34	153	36
66	146	32	150	32	154	34	158	36
67	149	32	154	32	159	34	162	36
68	154	32	159	32	164	34	167	36
69	158	32	163	32	168	34	172	36
70	163	32	168	32	173	34	177	36
71	167	32	172	32	177	34	182	36
72	172	32	177	32	183	34	188	36
73	177	32	182	32	188	34	193	36
74	183	32	189	32	194	34	198	36
75	188	32	194	32	200	34	204	36
76	194	32	200	32	206	34	209	36
77	199	32	205	32	211	34	215	36
78	204	32	210	32	216	34	220	36
79	209	32	215	32	222	34	226	36
80	214	32	220	32	227	34	232	36

SOURCE: Headquarters, Department of the Army, 2007.

NOTES: The maximum allowed body fat percentages for male and female NPS enlistees ages 17–20 were 24 and 30, respectively, prior to July 2006. Chapter Two describes the de facto application of this standard in July 2005.

Table A.2
Proportion Eligible for ARMS, Pounds Overweight, Percentage Over–Body Fat, Proportion Who Took ARMS, and Proportion Who Passed ARMS, by MEPS

MEPS	Proportion Eligible for ARMS	Pounds Overweight	Percentage Over–Body Fat	Proportion Who Took ARMS	Proportion Who Passed ARMS	Number of Applicants
Spokane	0.021	30.9	2.1	1.000	0.500	580
Pittsburgh	0.056	35.5	2.1	0.943	0.485	1,243
Chicago	0.107	37.3	2.4	0.938	0.709	1,504
San Antonio	0.087	33.7	2.0	0.929	0.639	1,778
Jackson	0.044	43.3	2.0	0.920	0.391	563
Syracuse	0.042	33.4	1.9	0.909	0.350	1,048
Seattle	0.087	34.6	2.2	0.908	0.624	1,386
Milwaukee	0.057	37.3	2.2	0.901	0.580	1,946
Buffalo	0.072	33.1	2.5	0.889	0.825	629
Omaha	0.052	30.4	1.9	0.875	0.143	610
Sacramento	0.069	32.0	1.8	0.872	0.706	1,132
Atlanta	0.071	38.5	2.2	0.867	0.480	1,601
Amarillo	0.061	27.0	2.1	0.867	0.513	733
Phoenix	0.070	34.5	2.1	0.866	0.684	2,238
New Orleans	0.075	38.9	2.2	0.864	0.544	879
Detroit	0.063	31.1	1.7	0.861	0.254	1,254
Montgomery	0.104	33.1	2.0	0.858	0.825	2,490
Columbus	0.062	34.7	1.9	0.857	0.417	2,258
Houston	0.103	42.4	2.3	0.856	0.748	3,185
Portland, Oregon	0.039	35.6	1.7	0.852	0.462	1,571
Kansas City	0.056	33.3	1.9	0.852	0.609	2,401
San Diego	0.077	40.1	2.5	0.841	0.621	894
Baltimore	0.042	43.7	2.4	0.826	0.658	2,179
Portland, Maine	0.057	45.2	2.5	0.824	0.714	592
Oakland	0.057	39.2	2.2	0.823	0.548	1,986
Albuquerque	0.032	24.8	2.0	0.812	0.308	498
Sioux Falls	0.049	26.7	1.4	0.812	0.231	329
Nashville	0.054	28.5	1.8	0.803	0.298	1,316
Butte	0.052	34.1	2.2	0.800	0.450	482
Anchorage	0.077	32.2	2.6	0.800	0.600	324
Minneapolis	0.077	38.4	2.1	0.786	0.545	910
Salt Lake City	0.055	32.3	1.7	0.776	0.212	1,211
Beckley	0.058	32.8	2.0	0.771	0.182	829

Table A.2—Continued

MEPS	Proportion Eligible for ARMS	Pounds Overweight	Percentage Over–Body Fat	Proportion Who Took ARMS	Proportion Who Passed ARMS	Number of Applicants
Knoxville	0.030	35.3	2.1	0.767	0.455	1,012
Raleigh	0.089	33.6	2.1	0.760	0.504	2,064
St. Louis	0.052	30.5	1.7	0.748	0.358	2,463
Charlotte	0.044	34.1	1.8	0.743	0.275	1,578
Indianapolis	0.039	37.2	2.0	0.741	0.372	1,470
Boise	0.026	34.3	1.5	0.737	0.071	735
Los Angeles	0.057	31.2	2.0	0.735	0.488	2,972
Fort Jackson	0.068	31.0	2.1	0.732	0.326	1,811
Lansing	0.084	34.5	1.9	0.732	0.750	1,959
Cleveland	0.050	32.4	2.0	0.731	0.327	1,337
Louisville	0.055	34.8	1.9	0.727	0.250	1,005
Springfield	0.060	35.7	2.1	0.721	0.341	1,024
Dallas	0.072	33.4	2.0	0.709	0.432	3,699
Albany	0.040	23.4	2.2	0.704	0.263	674
Jacksonville	0.076	37.1	2.1	0.688	0.545	2,726
New York	0.060	34.5	1.9	0.688	0.737	2,389
Denver	0.036	23.6	1.5	0.686	0.146	1,943
Oklahoma City	0.044	27.3	2.0	0.675	0.167	1,831
Tampa	0.045	29.1	1.7	0.675	0.427	2,830
Des Moines	0.025	36.7	2.2	0.667	0.286	828
Philadelphia	0.059	37.6	2.0	0.658	0.400	1,298
Harrisburg	0.027	40.3	2.1	0.658	0.480	1,384
Richmond	0.042	34.2	2.4	0.654	0.725	1,850
El Paso	0.046	27.0	1.7	0.652	0.200	498
Boston	0.020	37.9	2.0	0.640	0.400	1,250
Memphis	0.034	38.6	1.9	0.640	0.125	732
Honolulu	0.039	40.6	1.8	0.611	0.000	458
San Juan	0.027	29.6	1.6	0.600	0.083	729
Miami	0.016	48.7	2.1	0.560	0.286	1,519
Shreveport	0.031	36.2	2.1	0.545	0.389	1,059
Little Rock	0.054	27.5	1.7	0.475	0.107	1,091
Fargo	0.058	26.2	1.5	0.438	0.143	275

NOTES: The sample is limited to NPS regular Army applicants who applied to one of the eight early MEPS between February 2006 and September 2007; to one of the six study site MEPS between October 2006 and September 2007 (the ARMS-specific data we received for these MEPS did not cover the pre–October 2006 period); or to the other MEPS between April 2006 and September 2007. Chapter Two describes additional sample restrictions.

References

Asch, Beth J., Christopher A. Buck, Jacob Alex Klerman, Meredith Kleykamp, and David S. Loughran, *Military Enlistment of Hispanic Youth: Obstacles and Opportunities*, Santa Monica, Calif.: RAND Corporation, MG-773-OSD, 2009. As of May 20, 2011: http://www.rand.org/pubs/monographs/MG773.html

Bedno, Sheryl A., Christine E. Lang, William E. Daniell, Andrew R. Wiesen, Bennett Datu, and David W. Niebuhr, "Association of Weight at Enlistment with Enrollment in the Army Weight Control Program and Subsequent Attrition in the Assessment of Recruit Motivation and Strength," *Military Medicine*, Vol. 175, No. 3, March 2010, pp. 1–6.

Bedno, Sheryl A., Yuanzhang Li, Weiwei Han, David N. Cowan, Christine T. Scott, Melinda A. Cavicchia, and David W. Niebuhr, "Exertional Heat Illness Among Overweight U.S. Army Recruits in Basic Training," *Aviation, Space, and Environmental Medicine*, Vol. 81, No. 2, February 2010, pp. 107–111.

Headquarters, Department of the Army, *The Army Weight Control Program*, AR 600-9, Washington, D.C., November 27, 2006.

———, *Standards of Medical Fitness*, AR 40-501, Washington, D.C., December 14, 2007.

Niebuhr, David W., Christine T. Scott, Timothy E. Powers, Yuanzhang Li, Weiwei Han, Amy M. Milikan, and Margot R. Krauss, "Assessment of Recruit Motivation and Strength Study: Preaccession Physical Fitness Assessment Predicts Early Attrition," *Military Medicine,* Vol. 173, No. 6, June 2008, pp. 555–562.

Niebuhr, David W., Christine T. Scott, Yuanzhang Li, Sheryl A. Bedno, Weiwei Han, and Timothy E. Powers, "Preaccession Fitness and Body Composition as Predictors of Attrition in U.S. Army Recruits," *Military Medicine*, Vol. 174, No. 7, July 2009, pp. 695–701.

Office of the Under Secretary of Defense, Personnel and Readiness, *Population Representation in the Military Services: Fiscal Year 2004*, May 2006.

———, *Population Representation in the Military Services: Fiscal Year 2007*, undated.

U.S. Department of Labor, Bureau of Labor Statistics, "Local Area Unemployment Statistics," web page, undated.